The Smoking Fifties

How Once We Looked: Photographs of the Past

michael philip manheim
PHOTOGRAPHY

SEE-SAW

Editions

ALSO BY MICHAEL PHILIP MANHEIM

IN A LABYRINTH
LAST HOUSE STANDING
WHERE MY SPIRIT GUIDES US
SEE-SAW, A Sampler

For further information or permissions, including the leasing of reproduction rights, contact Michael Philip Manheim at http://www.michaelphilipmanheim.com/MPM-contact_form.php

Book design and layout: J. Putnam Design www.jputnamdesign.com

Printed in the United States of America.

ISBN 978-0-9844803-4-0

Cover photograph: Girl Smoking ©1959
Back cover photograph: Hats on Sale ©1956

"I'm inspired that you stood alone to pursue your photography and explore your passion."

Ashley Cheak, photography student at Stivers School for the Arts in Dayton, Ohio, 2017

Part of a retrospective series of my work which is dedicated to Stephen B. Jareckie,

The Smoking Fifties is a chapter in this series of nostalgic photography

and is dedicated to my sister, a physical therapy guru, author and teacher,

Carol J. Manheim,

who shared so many eras with me.

Foreword

Michael Philip Manheim began his photography career shooting black-and-white film, street documentary style, in Ohio in the early 1950s. By the end of the decade, he moved on, to Philadelphia, then Boston, working professionally as a freelance photojournalist by 1969.

Michael's photography from this period is wonderfully telling: the haircuts, the style of clothing, the little details in the background that communicate where and when his pictures were made. These bits of evidence captured in combination with his careful attention to gestures and expressions, round out a full exploration of a specific time and place in human existence.

Over the next few decades, Michael's photographic interests and the resulting images radically evolved. Still passionate about capturing a sense of place and humanity, by the 1990s he turned away from straight realism and toward the conceptual. This later work utilized a multiple exposure technique that enabled him to create more primal, spiritual imagery. He has shown these pictures extensively. Yet Michael's photojournalistic images, generated out of the same fascination with his subjects, and utilizing the same honed skills and expressive approach, have only resurfaced recently.

Michael is now honoring the vintage 8x10 silver prints of the documentary work in his archives by creating editions of large-scale archival prints from carefully selected and scanned original negatives. I am delighted to see him return to this treasured material and share it here.

— **Jennifer Uhrhane**

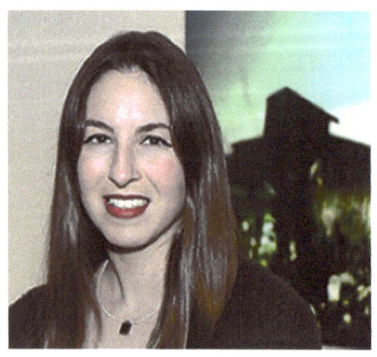

Photograph by Caleb Cole

Jennifer Uhrhane is a curatorial and collections management consultant. She covers a range of freelance projects from curating exhibitions and registrarial work to keeping private collections organized and finding homes for artists' estates. Her most recent success is the placement of the Lucien Aigner photography archive, shared by the Yale University Art Gallery, the Beinecke Rare Book & Manuscript Library at Yale, and the Addison Gallery of American Art at Phillips Academy, Andover.

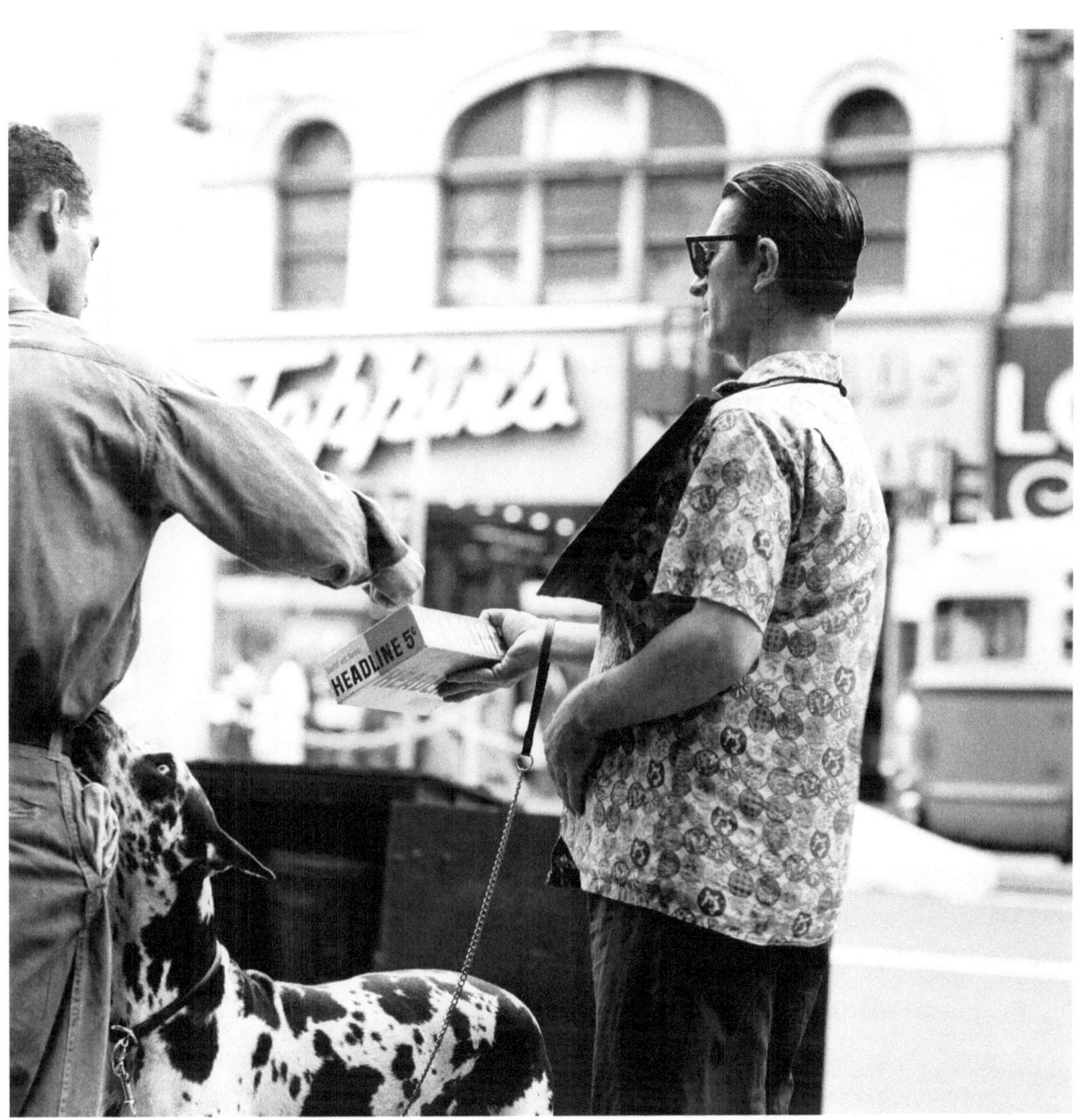

Blind *Philadelphia, Pennsylvania 1958*

The Smoking Fifties
Looking at my world in the 1950s

After World War II ended in 1945, factories were smoking. That was slang for back into consumer production, but literally as well. Rationing had ended, and the United States economy shifted more to goods and services for civilians. Despite another war, this time in Korea, running from 1950 to 1953, peacetime manufacturing was in full swing.

Our world was radically changing. I captured that changing world with my cameras.

My passion for photography was smoking, too, when I entered Alliance High School in 1955. Leland H. "Whit" Whitaker not only taught photography there, he also created a kind of fiefdom where we were encouraged to explore our craft and our world. Here I found my kindred souls.

Photography became an outlet not only for creative expression, but for dealing with feelings in what now seems like a straitlaced decade. We didn't directly express feelings in my family, to be sure; we were expected to know what the other person was thinking. I was also expected to stay in the family clothing store business. I spent much of the first 25 years of my life devoted to that enterprise.

Photography was understood to be my enthusiasm, indulged on the side. However, as I started winning contests, I developed a fervor that wouldn't quit. Developing film and creating prints gave me an essential grounding in the technical aspects of photography. At first enamored of the equipment, I came to regard cameras as tools that would serve my sense of composition, lighting and empathy. Embracing the digital era has become the next logical step.

I still have vintage prints, those I created close to the time I developed my negatives. But now I collaborate on creating larger, pigmented ink-jet contemporary prints. These are just as archival but, with today's technology, tweaked into a pinpoint perfection that was not possible in earlier times.

Ah, it's a great time to be digitizing my archives!

— Michael Philip Manheim

American Steel Foundries in Alliance, Ohio was one of several local factories pushing ahead in a new era. On pouring days an acrid odor traveled miles from the industrial area downtown to the developing areas bordering Route 62, access to the outside world.

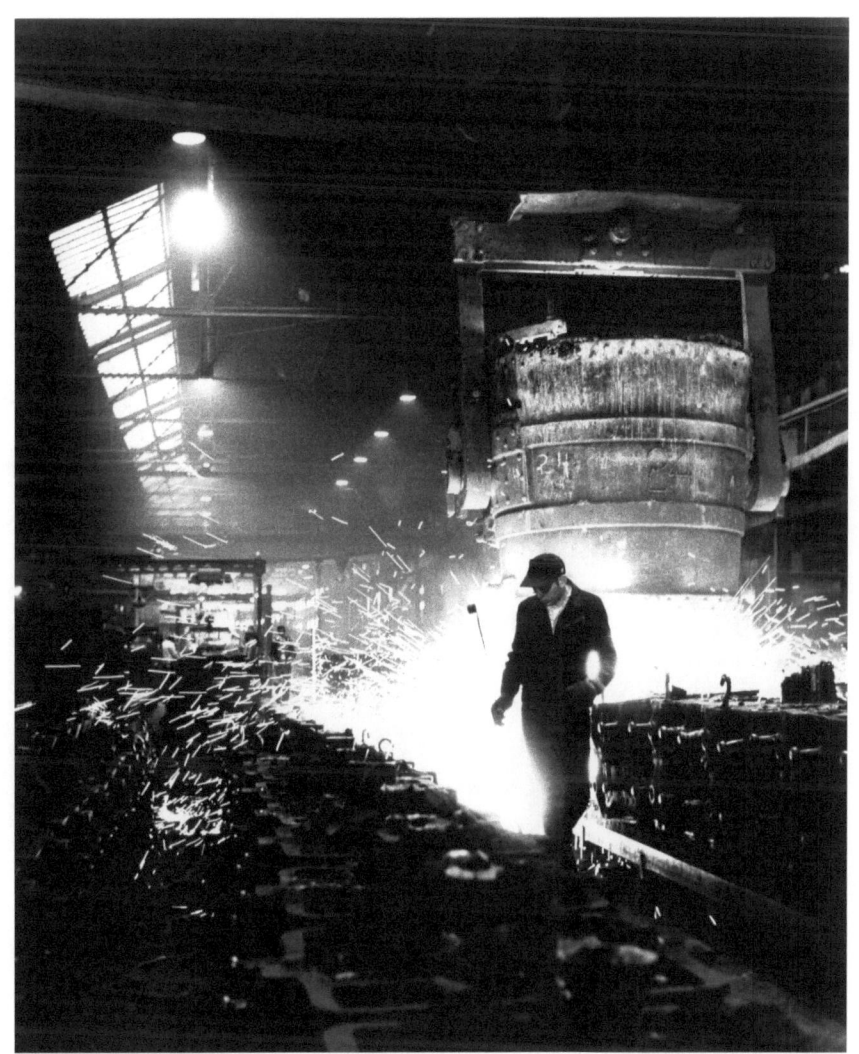

Steel Pouring *Alliance, Ohio 1957*

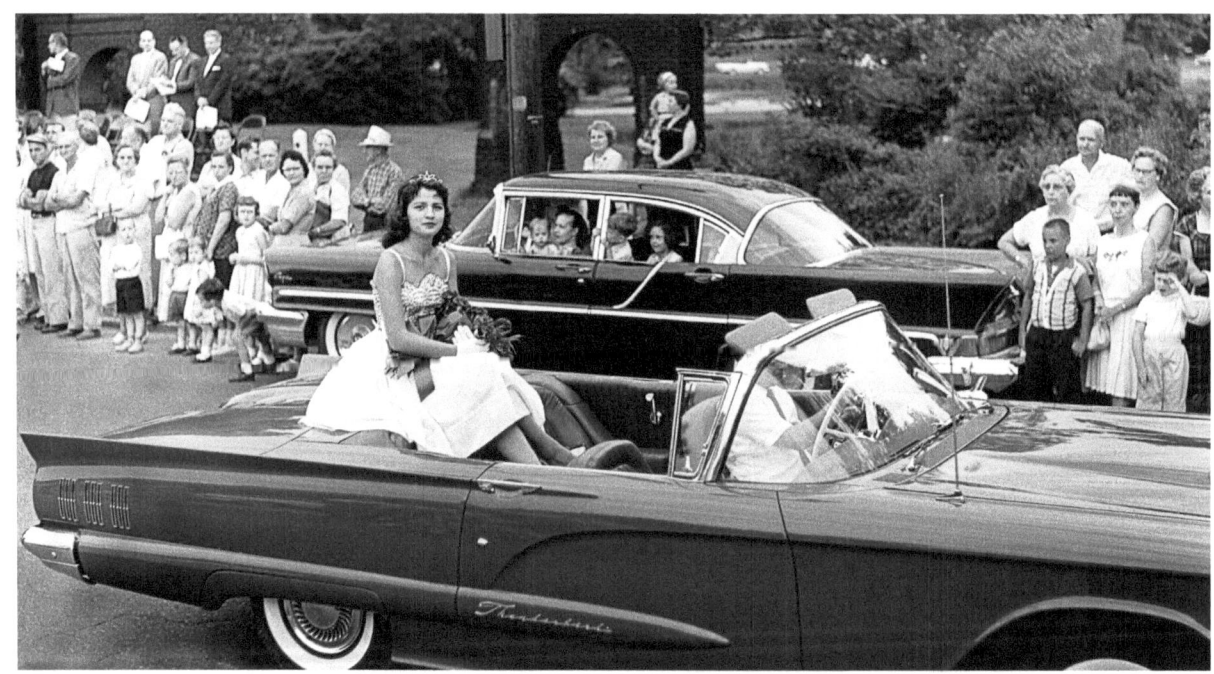

Teenage Queen *Alliance, Ohio 1959*

Women had proved themselves as test and delivery pilots, as shipbuilders, as workers on factory floors. But the military men were back, taking over their old jobs. Roles shifted once again, and were passed along to the new generation.

Symbolically, many females moved back into traditional roles of cheerleaders and majorettes, beauty queens and housewives, keeping homes and raising children. Women's career roles were limited, and included sales clerks, secretaries, assistants, nurses and schoolteachers.

Back to Gender Roles

There were exceptions. My friend Anne was born abroad. Both her father and mother had moved to Alliance to work as physicians. In the image opposite, you can see Anne's expression of ironical amusement at her assigned role as beauty queen. She went on to become a physician herself, an uncommon choice in those days.

As our attention shifted from the heroes of the armed forces, athletes became our newest heroes. They were encouraged by the young women in a traditional cheerleading role—for the time being.

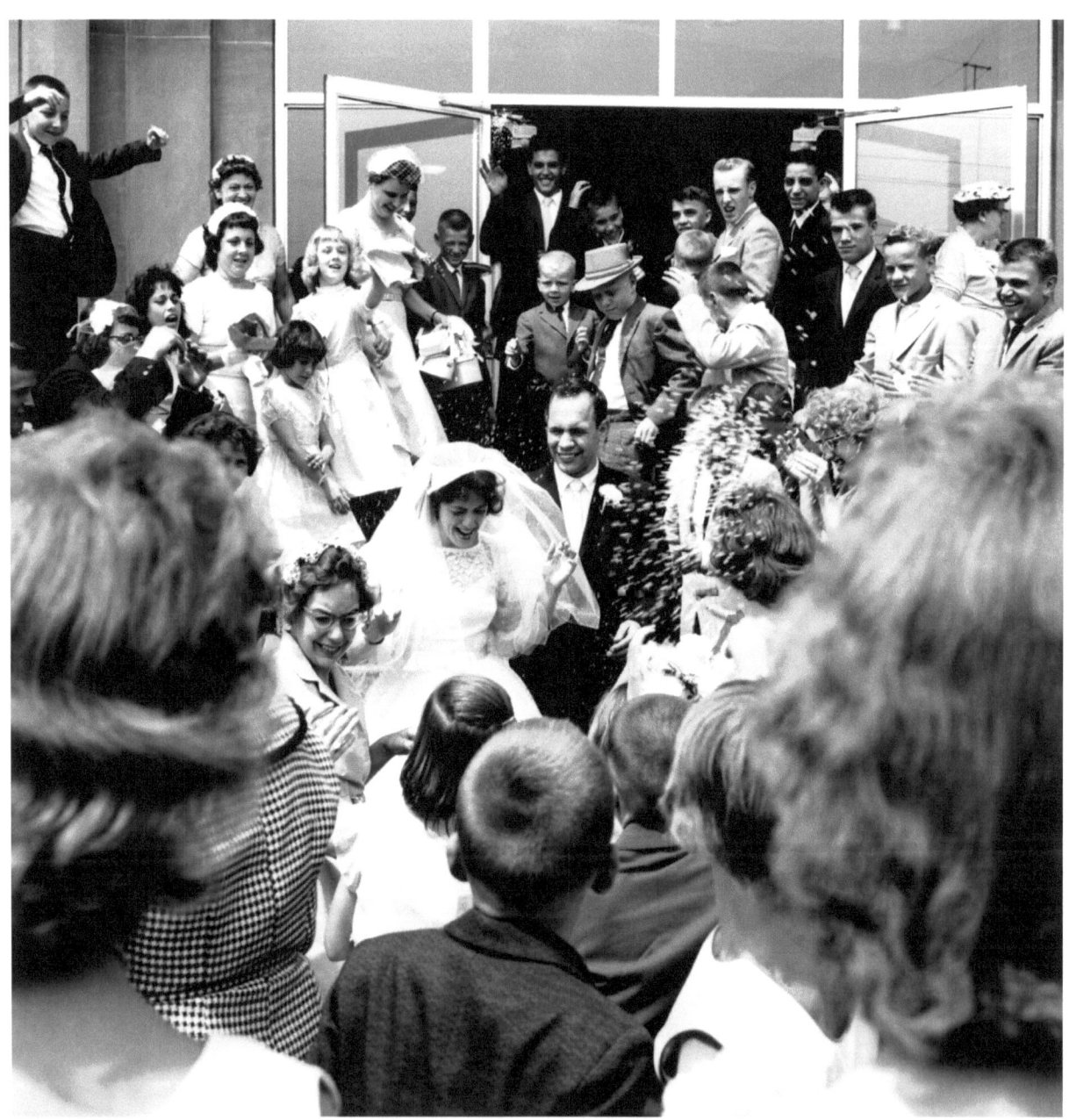

Wedding *Alliance, Ohio 1956*

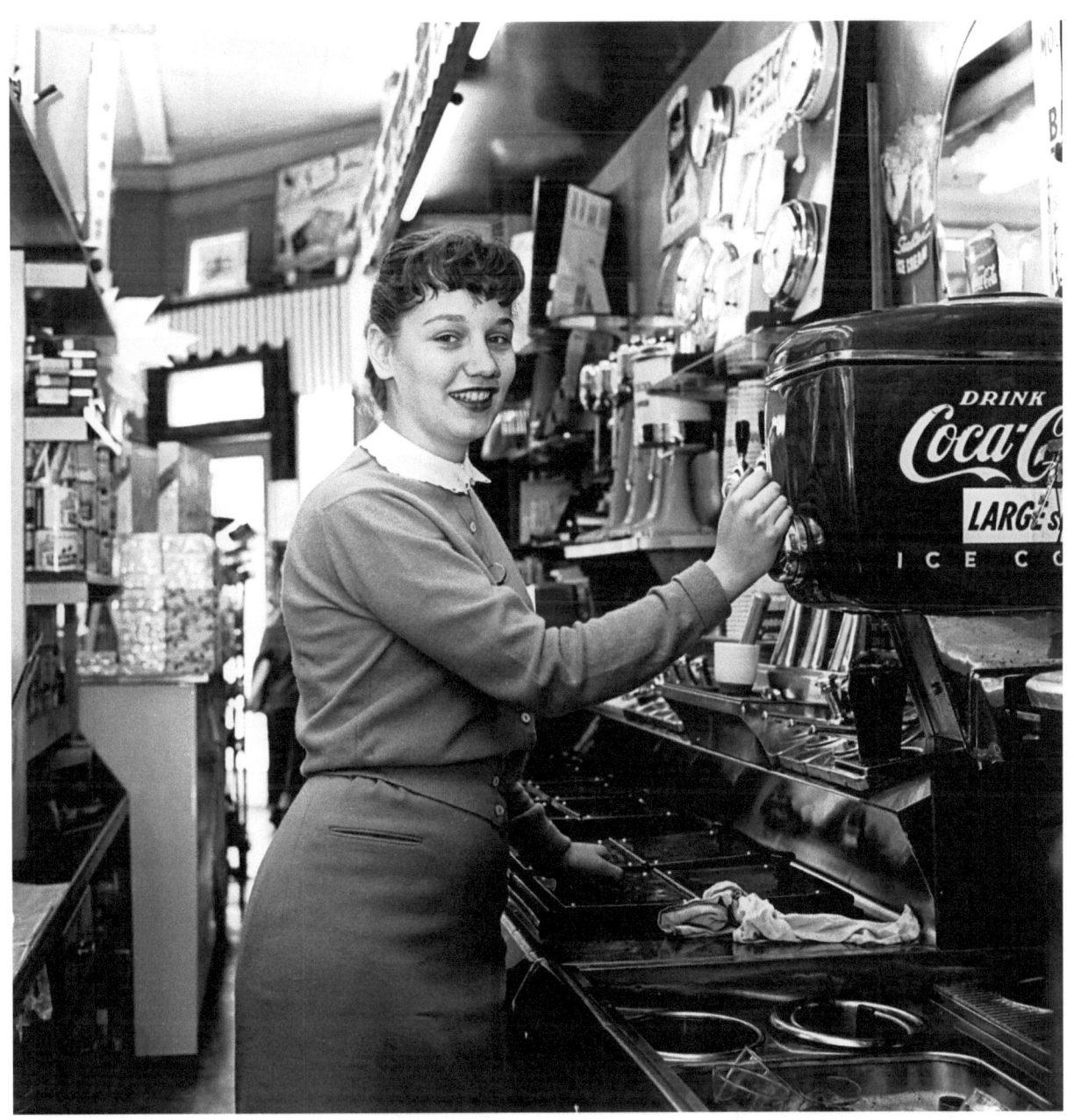

Soda Fountain *Alliance, Ohio 1956*

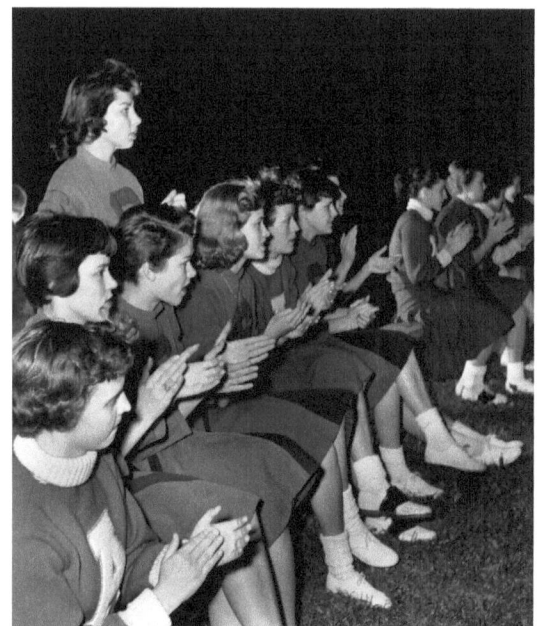

Cheerleaders *Alliance, Ohio 1957*

Daughters in cheerleader uniforms encourage their team, as their mothers might have done before the war. Sons played in the same stadium as their fathers once did.

In small-town Ohio pep rallies took on the sanctimonious air of church services, beginning with the school anthem and building up to "We're with you, team, so fight!" There were those, like me, who choked on mindless, shouted scripts. I was lucky to have discovered photography; I hid behind my camera and participated by documenting the scene.

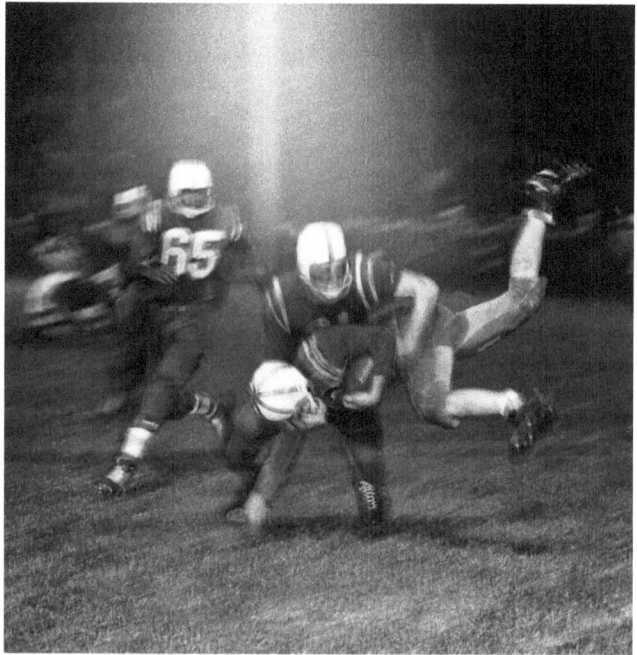

Tackle *Alliance, Ohio 1957*

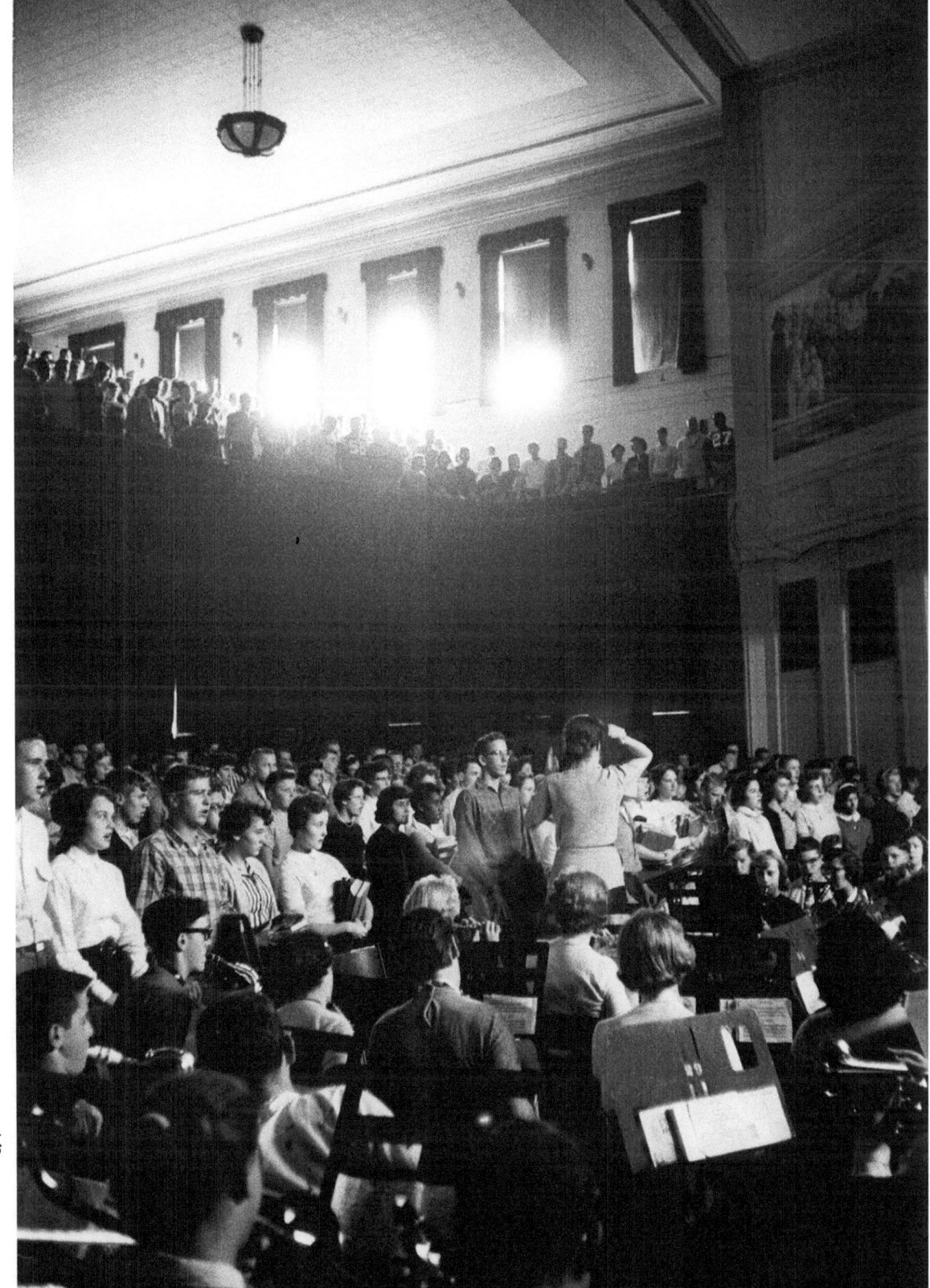

gh School Anthem
Alliance, Ohio 1956

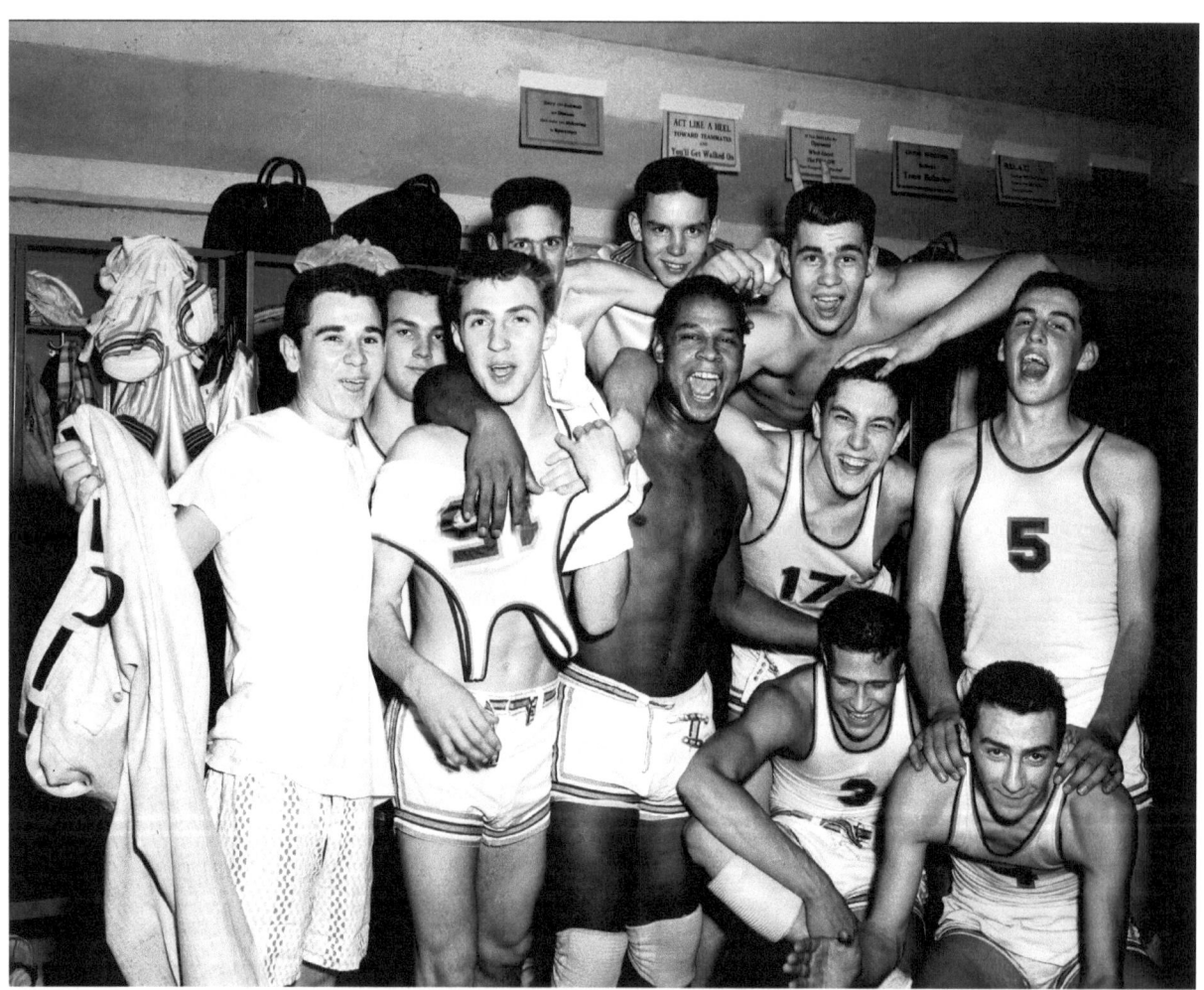

Celebrate! *Alliance, Ohio 1956*

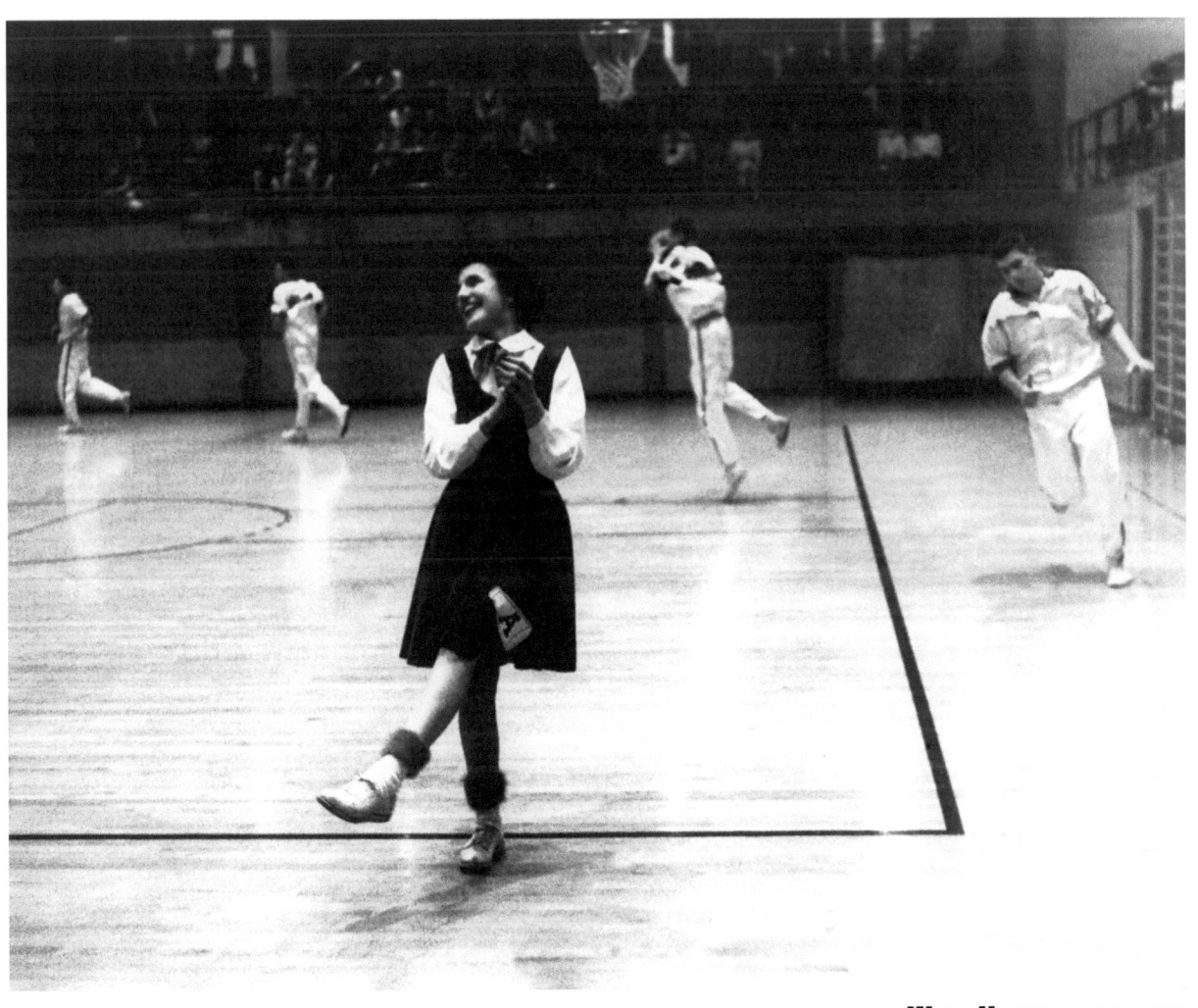

Warm Up *Alliance, Ohio 1956*

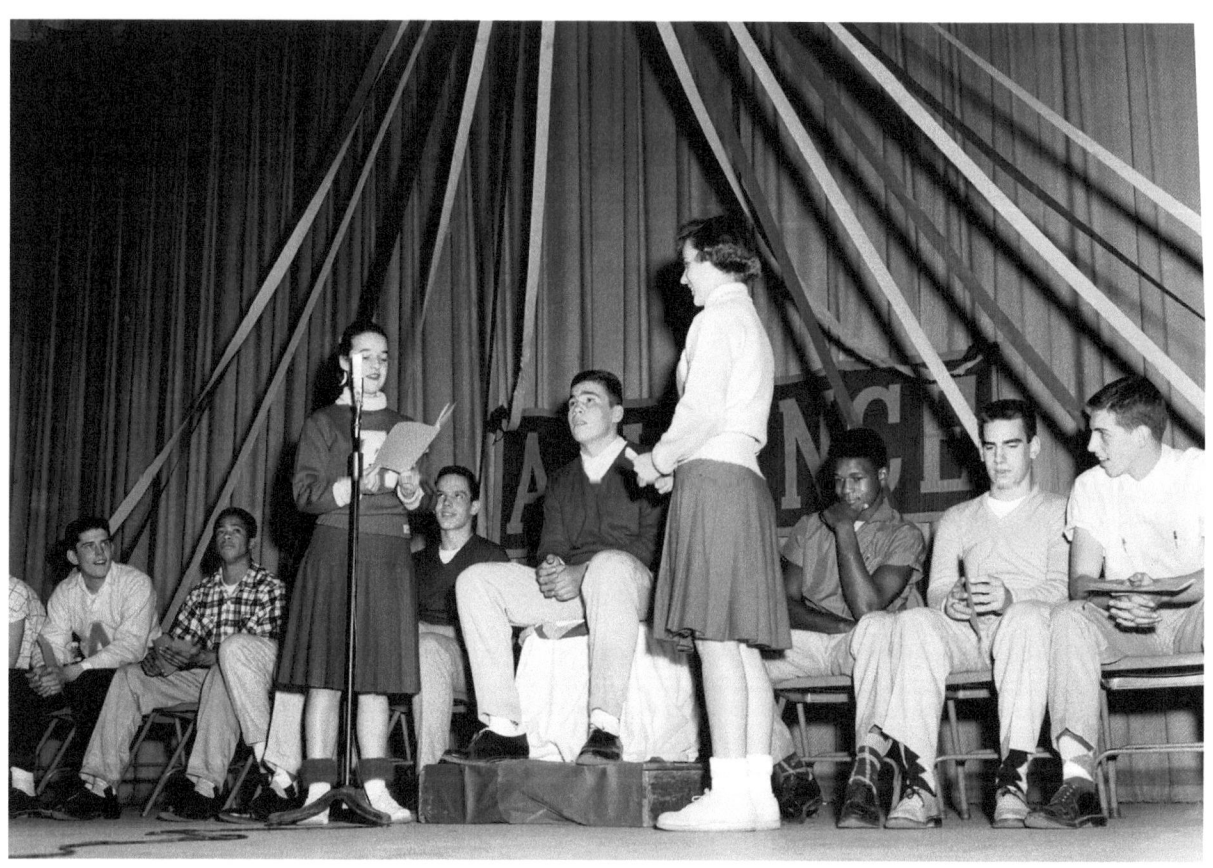

Basketball Awards *Alliance, Ohio 1956*

If you weren't an athlete or a cheerleader, you found other ways to fill your time and show off your skills. Bowling, target shooting, school-sanctioned clubs and activities were all available (including photography).

Irving Berlin's inspirational songs gave way to Glenn Miller, and "A String of Pearls" gave way to Bill Haley's "Rock Around the Clock." Elvis Presley came onto the scene, and Chuck Berry, Little Richard, and so many other rock 'n' rollers with their pioneering lyrics, music and body language. I traded in my violin for a saxophone as kids my age formed bands. I remember going with a new friend to his house after school, where he taught me to hum into my alto sax to play "Tequila!" Nearby, his father, back from his shift at the steel works, sat in his undershirt reading the newspaper.

What About the Rest of Us?

Here I was, oblivious as the rest, groomed to understudy a merchant father and to absorb both his and the community's values. So what was it like to live in a bubble? Some of us were aware of not really belonging to this community. That included not being part of the athletic set upon whom the town doted. Discrimination ranged from religion to popularity to prosperity to race; it was accepted that the railroad tracks leading to the train station downtown primarily divided the community into black and white. Both races acknowledged the racial discrimination and unfortunately, in retrospect, seemed to accept living with it. There was no segregation here, as in the South, where civil rights protest was awakening beginning in 1954.

For now, I was content to eagerly pursue my photography and to relate to the world through my cameras. I became a prize-winning spectator.

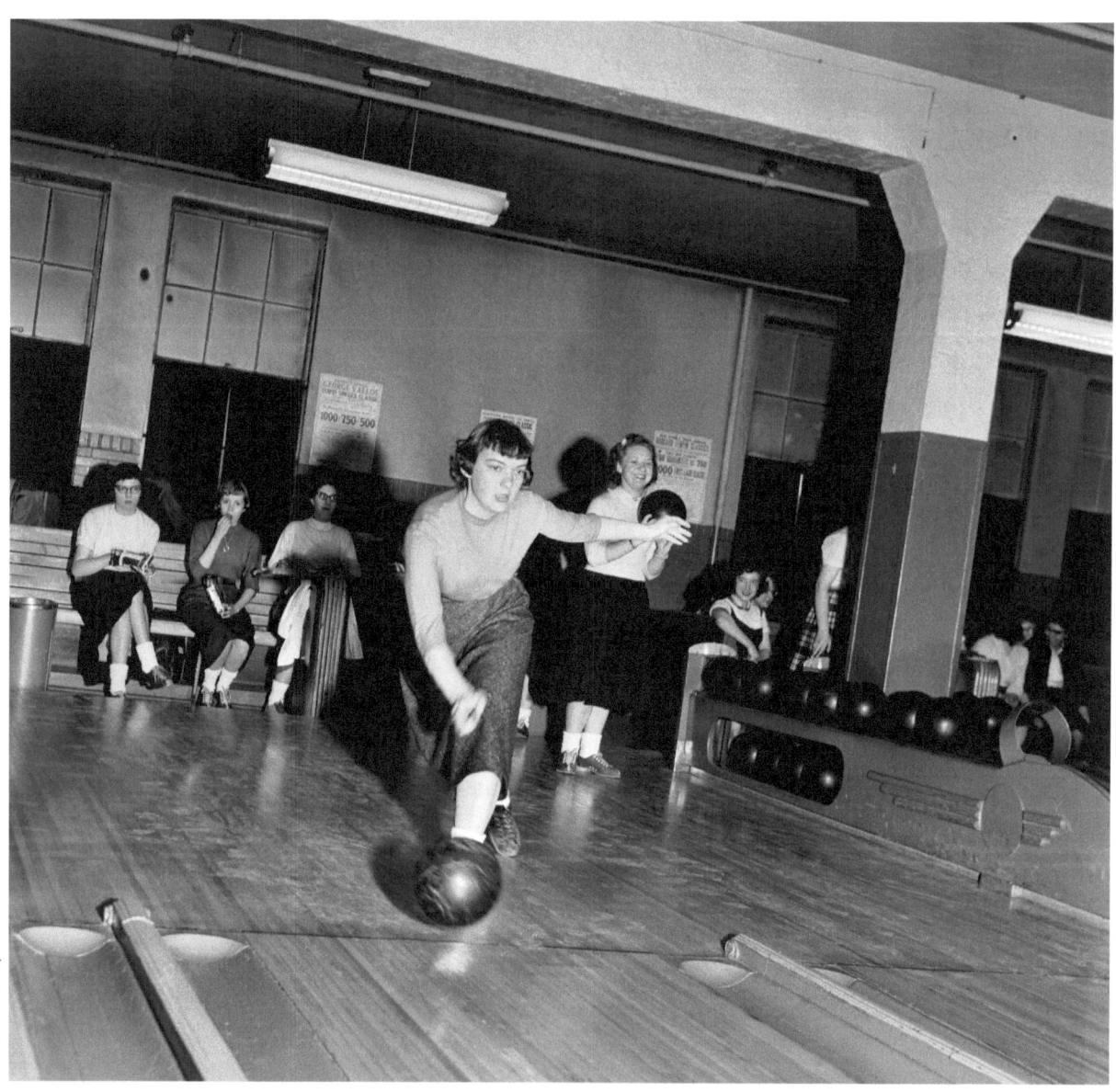

Bowling *Alliance, Ohio 1956*

I was a member of a target shooting extracurricular club, and won a Boy Scout marksman award. Besides my BB rifle and pistol, I owned two 22 caliber rifles. All this was typical for boys of that era, who naturally signed up as members of the NRA, a much more innocent organization of yesteryear! My club competed for and won trophies, but never would we shoot any living thing.

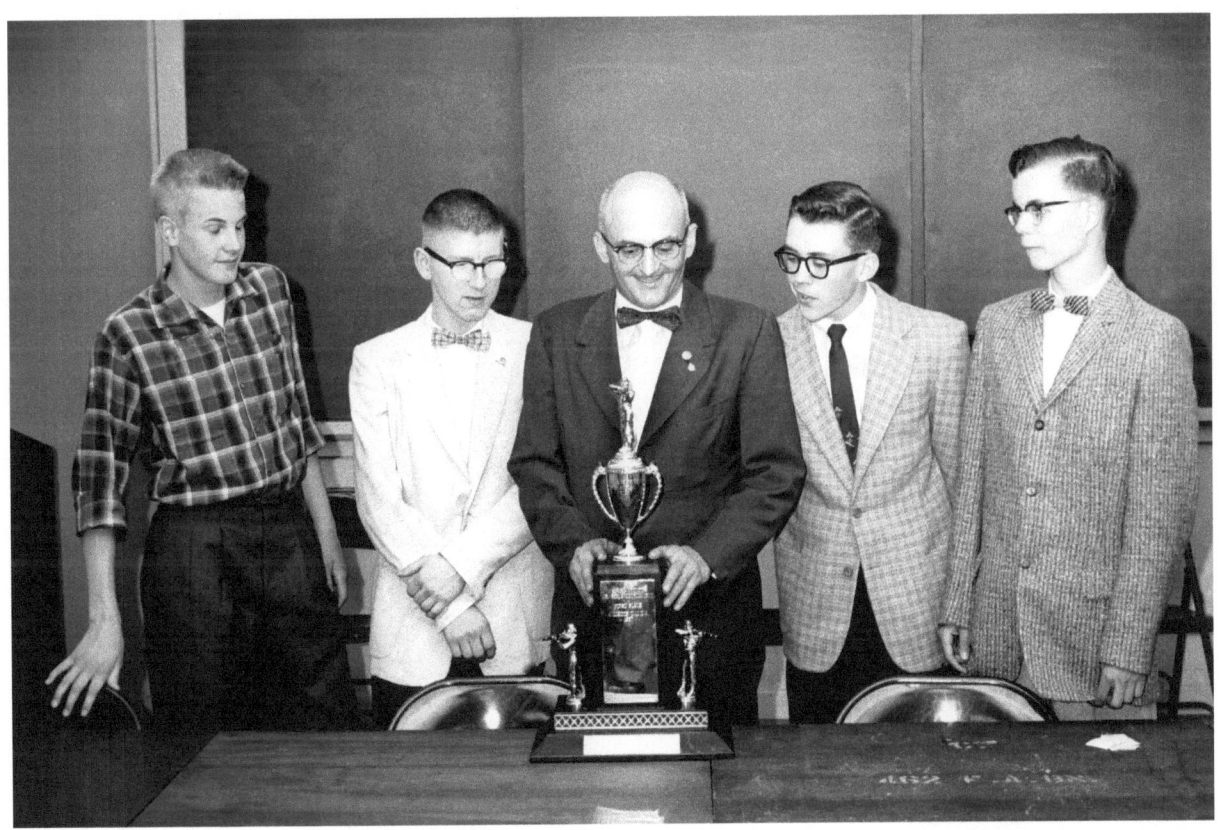

Marksmen *Alliance, Ohio 1955*

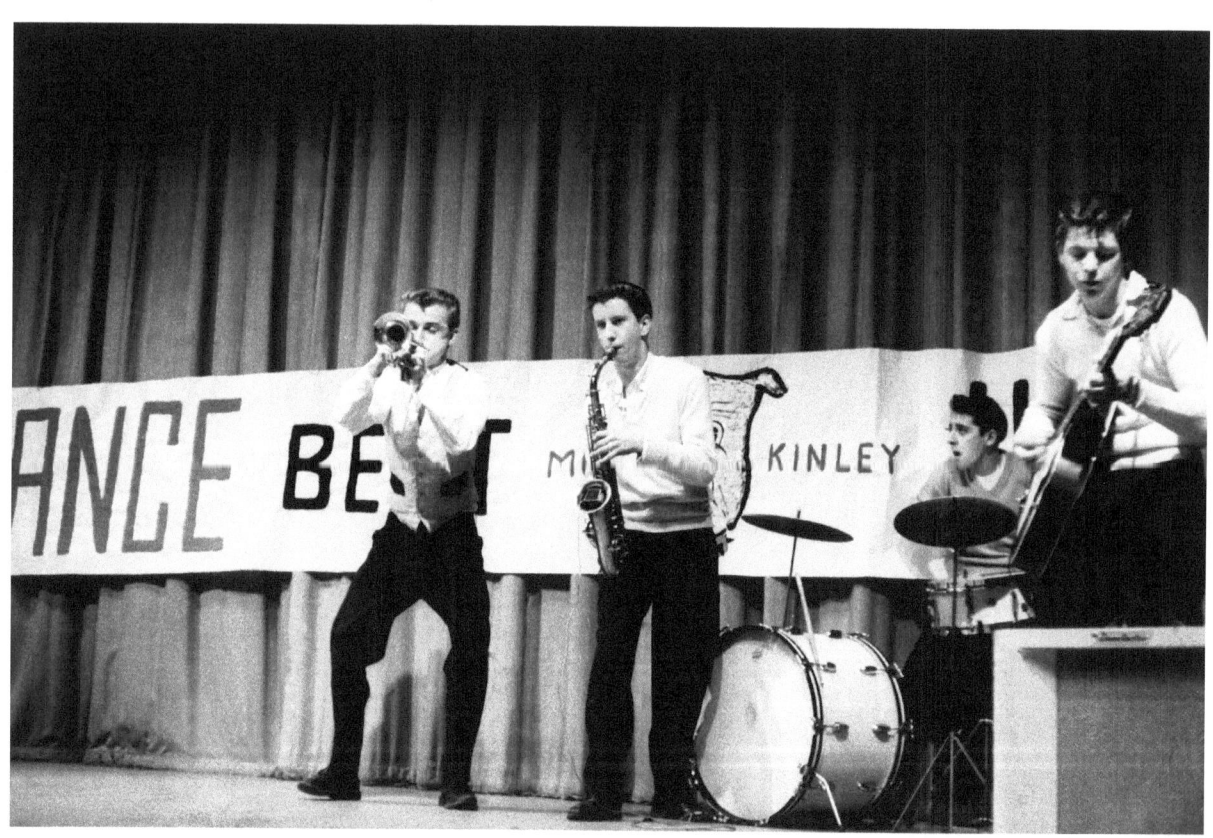

Rock 'n' Roll *Alliance, Ohio 1956*

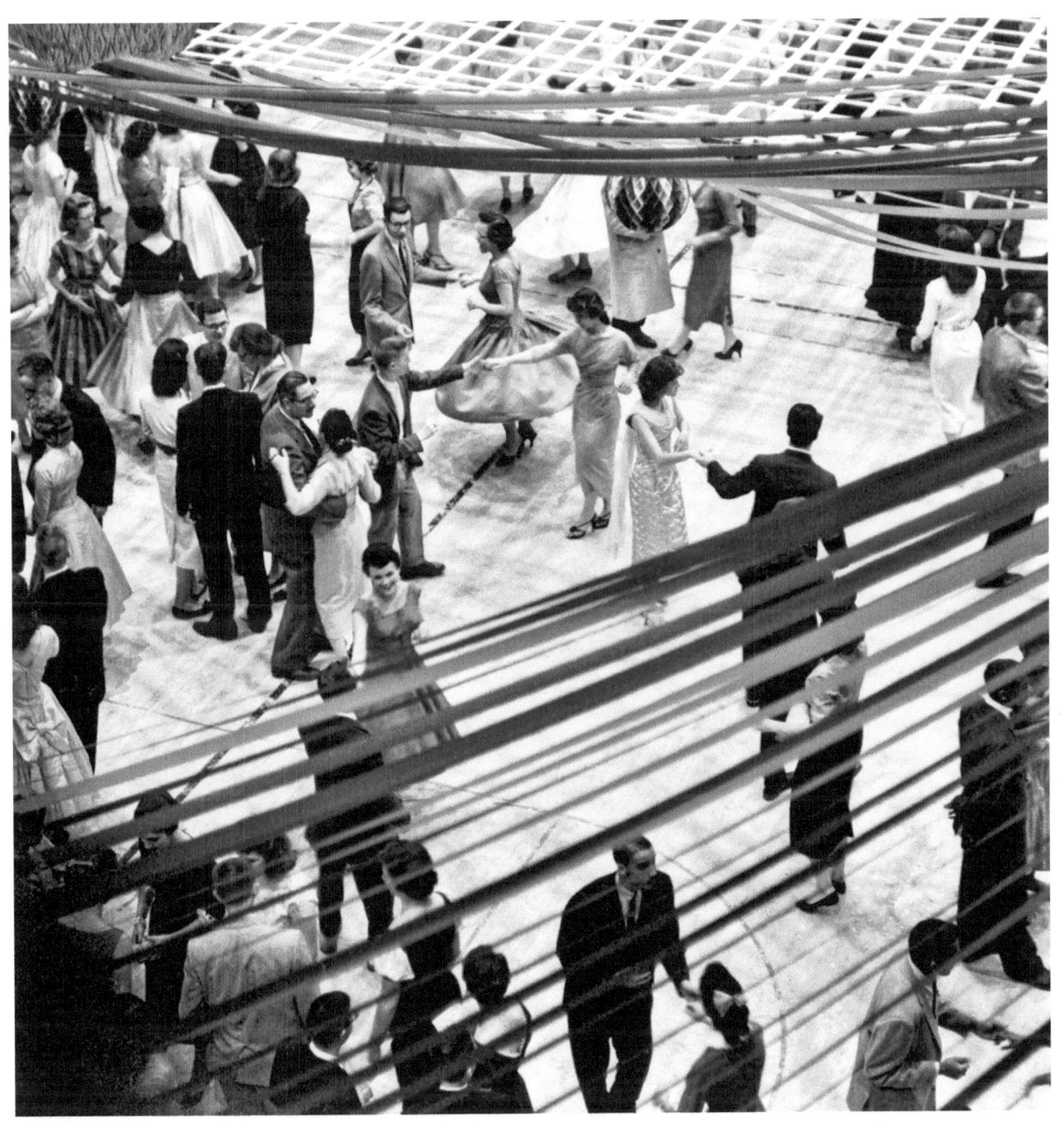

High School Prom *Alliance, Ohio 1957*

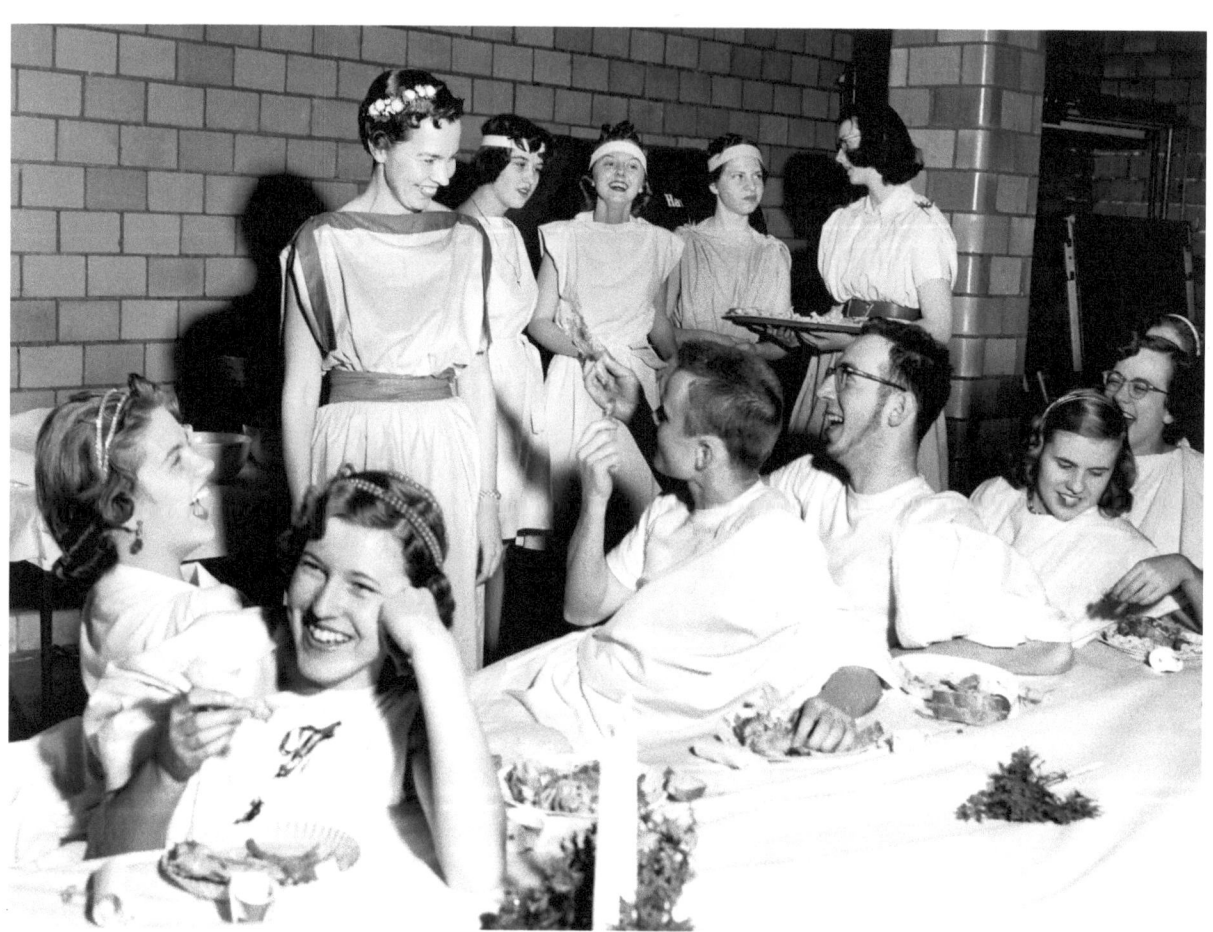

Latin Club *Alliance, Ohio 1956*

If you bought one of the first Cadillacs to roll off the post-war assembly lines, around 1946 or 1947, it might have been delivered with wooden bumpers. Automobile production was hard-pressed to keep up with a pent-up consumer demand. Sometimes auto dealers would take delivery of the chrome-plated steel bumpers later, as they became available, and replace the wooden ones.

Where we lived, you were known by your family car. One family always bought Pontiacs, another Chryslers. My father needed a Cadillac, and posed beside his new 1957 model on Main Street, where our family clothing store drew in the customers. Back then, Main Street was where you headed, coming to town to beef up your wardrobe, especially on sale days. Women in hats or babushkas, and men in fedoras or caps, returned with enthusiasm to the role of consumers.

Downtown

For me, the expectation was that I would give up photography and continue in the family business. I had worked part-time at the store since I was big enough to unfold gift boxes for the Christmas rush. I even attended the Wharton School of Finance and Commerce because it seemed to be my duty. But photography was my passion. After hours in the store, I worked on printing my photographs and creating queries to picture editors. I couldn't help it; I had to go after my own dream.

I became a full-time professional photographer when my second child was big enough to move to New England with the rest of us. I'm still at it, a late bloomer but I created a career—and am still delighted with my choice.

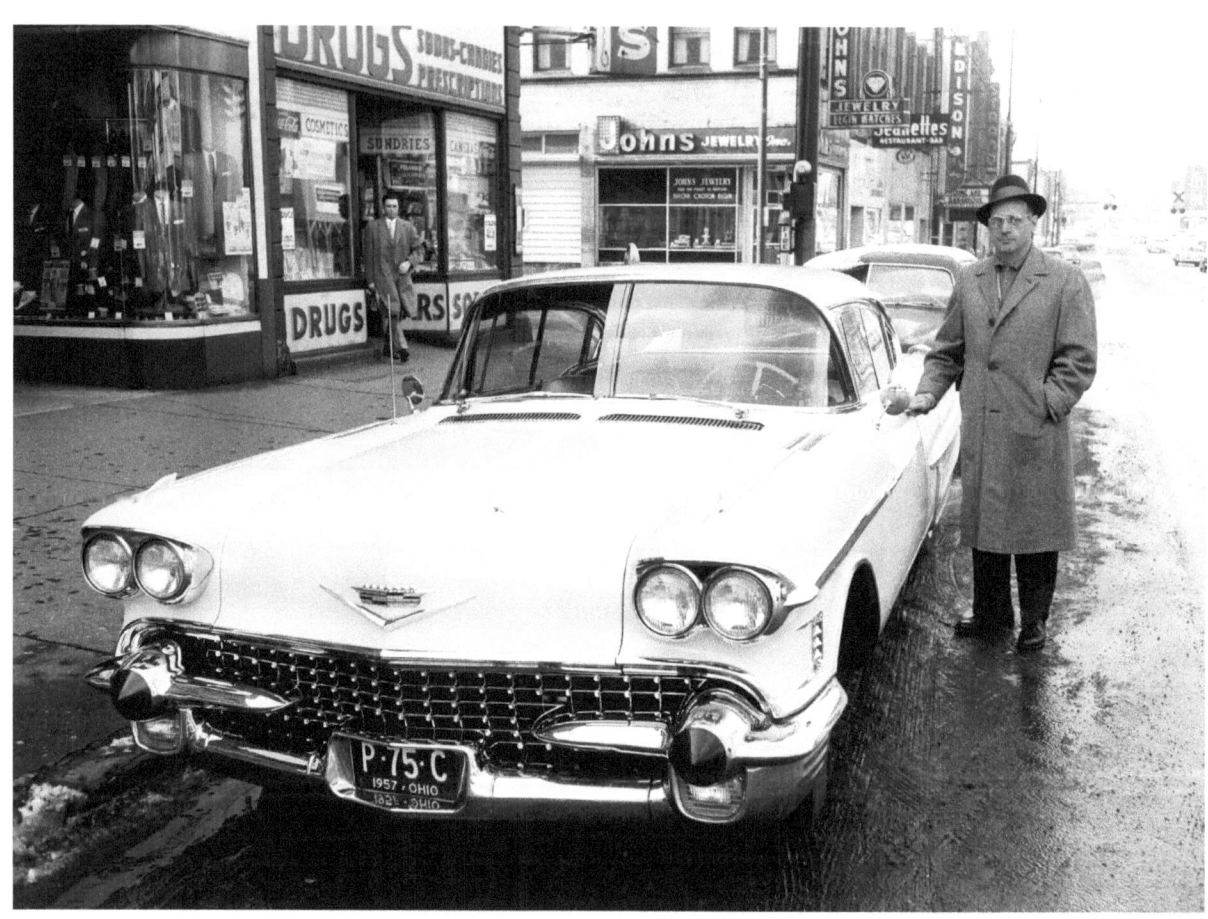

Success on Main Street *Alliance, Ohio 1957*

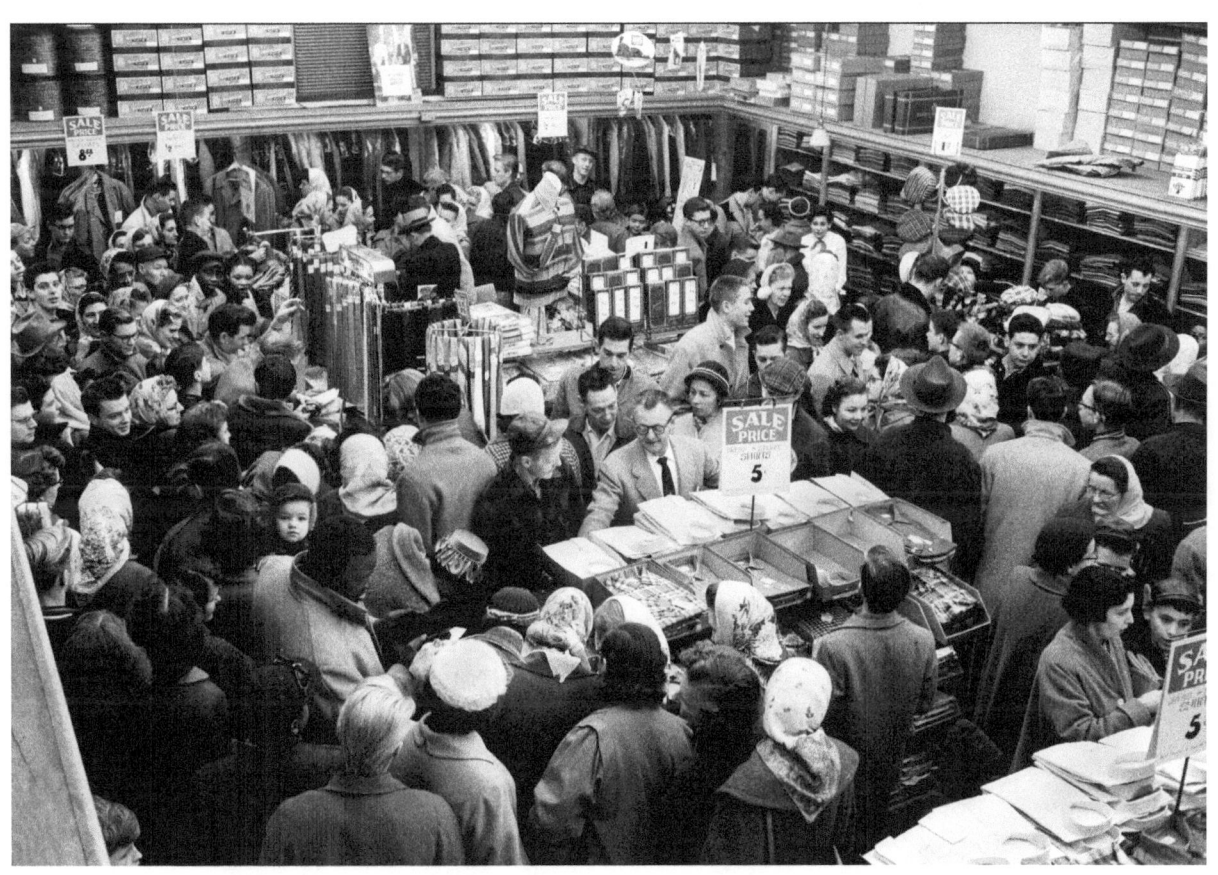

Sale Day Crowd *Alliance, Ohio 1957*

The Circus Came to Town

A long tradition came to an end on May 21, 2017 when Ringling Brothers and Barnum and Bailey Circus closed its final show, ending a continuous run of 146 years. Once appealing to crowds of every age and station, this "greatest show on earth" could not survive changing times.

The decline may have escalated when the show eliminated its elephant acts, but started with increasing competition. Many circuses around the world today display their own perspective. Olympic-quality athletes performing in Cirque du Soleil and other specialty shows offer their unique thrills to the crowds.

In this day of very different forms of entertainment, it is hard to imagine what a thrill it was when the old-fashioned big top circus came to town.

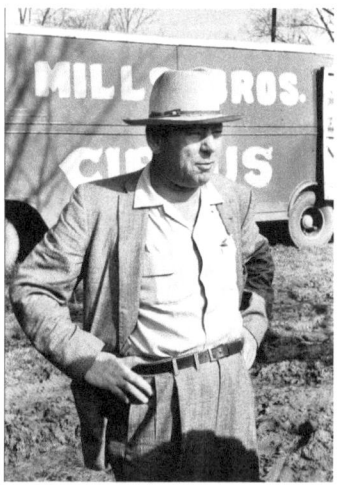

Circus Owner *Alliance, Ohio 1957*

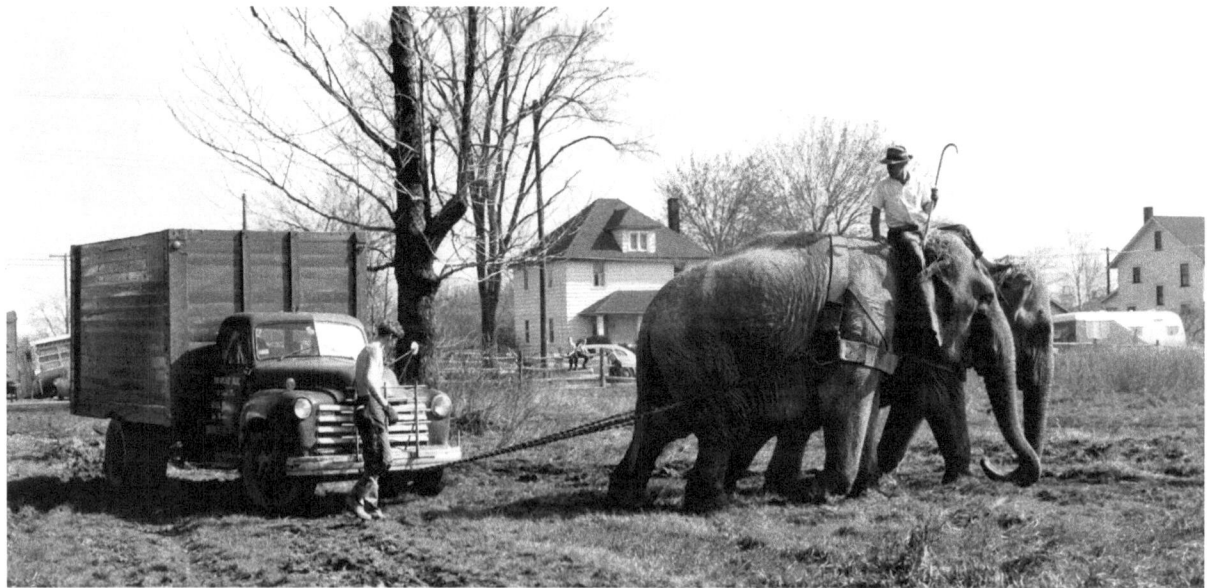

Setting Up the Circus *Alliance, Ohio 1957*

The Mills Brothers Circus would roll into Alliance, Ohio every spring, a much-anticipated annual event. Many townsfolk gathered to watch the excitement long before the actual show began. Seeing that circus setting up tents and services for the crews, performers, and animals was almost as much a spectacle as the show itself.

Advance people had posted directions for the drivers, and the circus components gathered on the West Vine Street Armory lot, not far from Main Street downtown. In 1957 it was a traditional circus, with elephants providing pulling power for trucks stuck in the mud. Tents were raised, performers settled into temporary quarters, people and

At the Circus *Alliance, Ohio 1957*

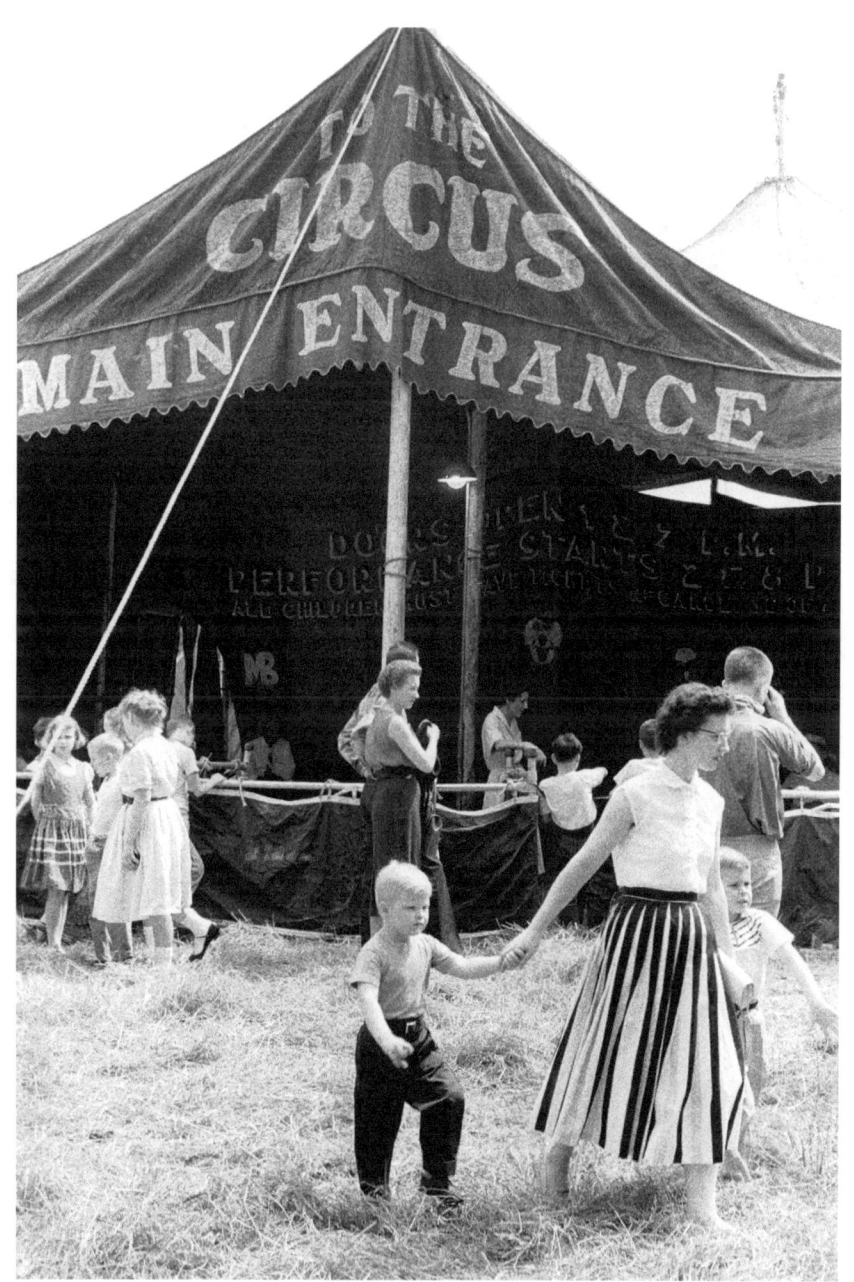

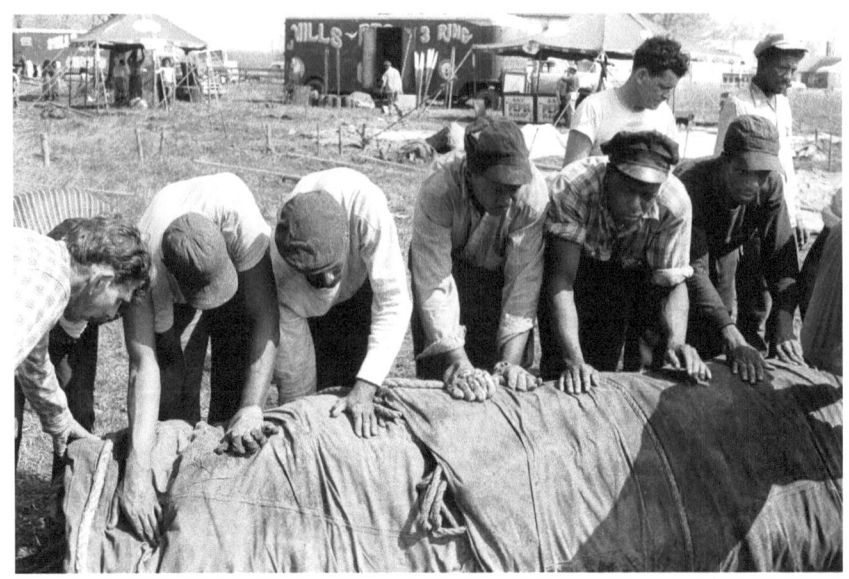

Unrolling the Big Top *Alliance, Ohio 1957*

animals were fed. With my photographer friends, Jim and Curt, we recorded the scene, each in our own way.

I was a witness, a budding photojournalist, knowing none of my subjects, eager to hone my skills. I was using a Leica IIIF, with distance and exposure pre-set, so that my reflexes could take over. This was practice I needed. *The Alliance Review* later produced some feature stories with my photographs.

The townsfolk were eager for entertainment once all was in place. We were, too, but the thrill was in developing our film, editing the images, and printing the best.

As *The Alliance Review* put it, "The Circus Travels on its Stomach":

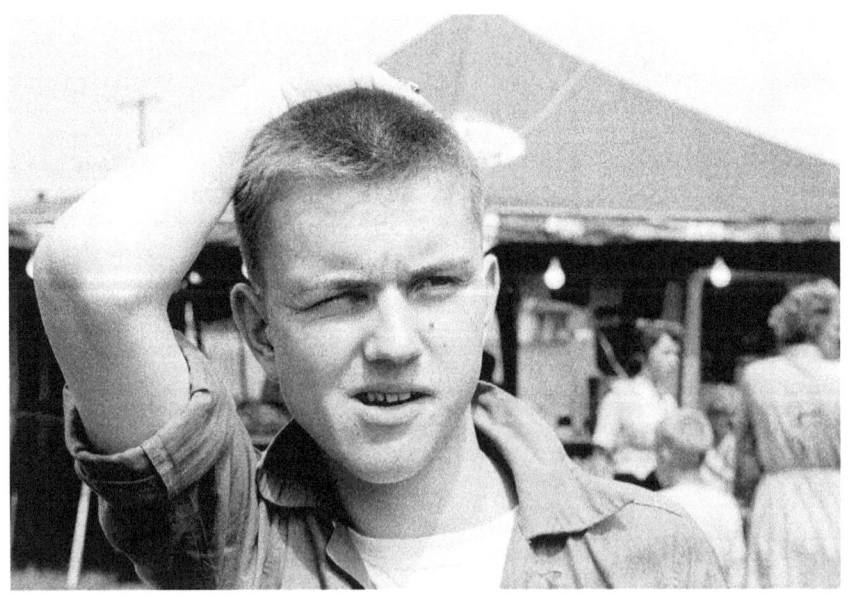

Curt at the Circus
Alliance, Ohio 1957

"The Mills Brothers may never have gone to West Point, but they know the problem of logistics, and have also developed it into a fine art. Food must be wholesome, nutritious, and must go a long way. The advance man has made provisions for its procurement 24 hours before the circus arrives"

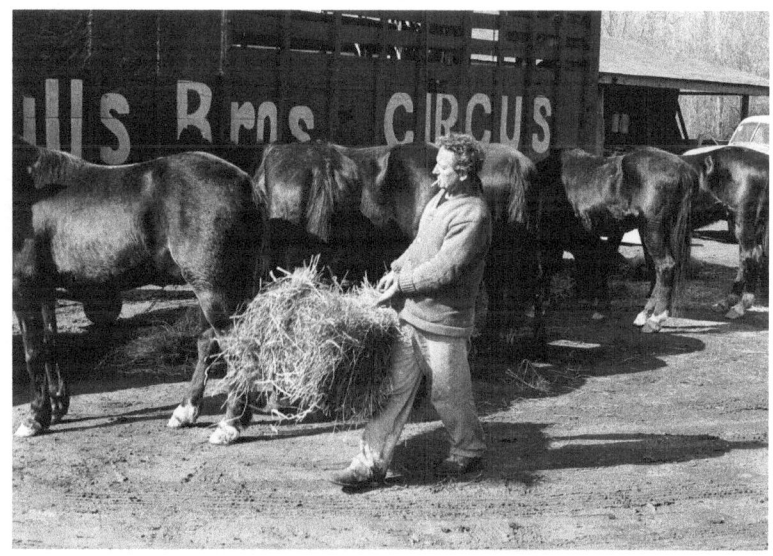

Feeding the Animals *Alliance, Ohio 1957*

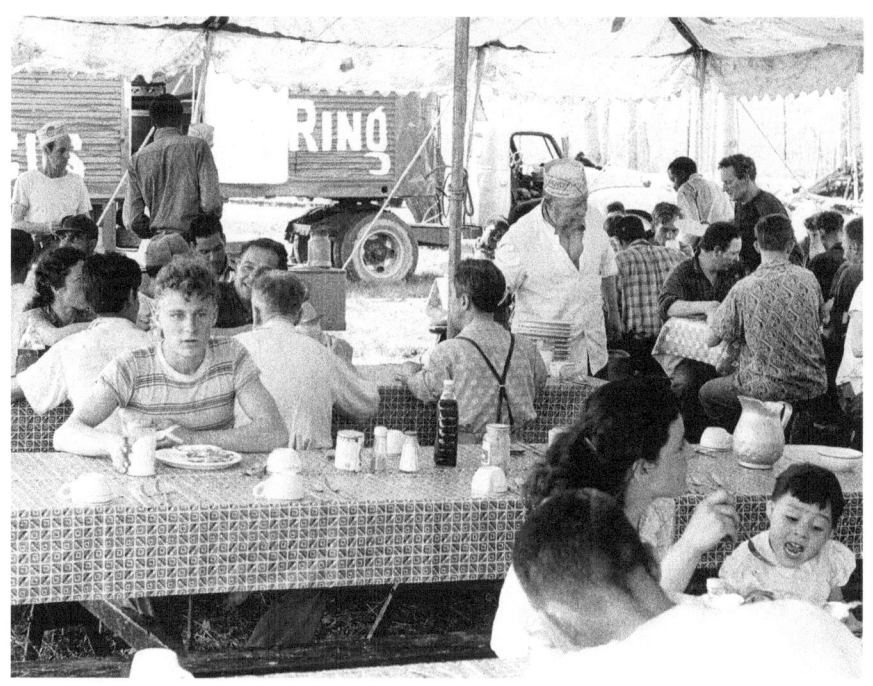

"Involved in the feeding of a circus are not only food and preparation, but the responsibility of getting it to the performers. This means transportation and many man-hours of work. They have done this for many years, tearing down and building up their 'kitchens' every day."

Feeding the People *Alliance, Ohio 1957*

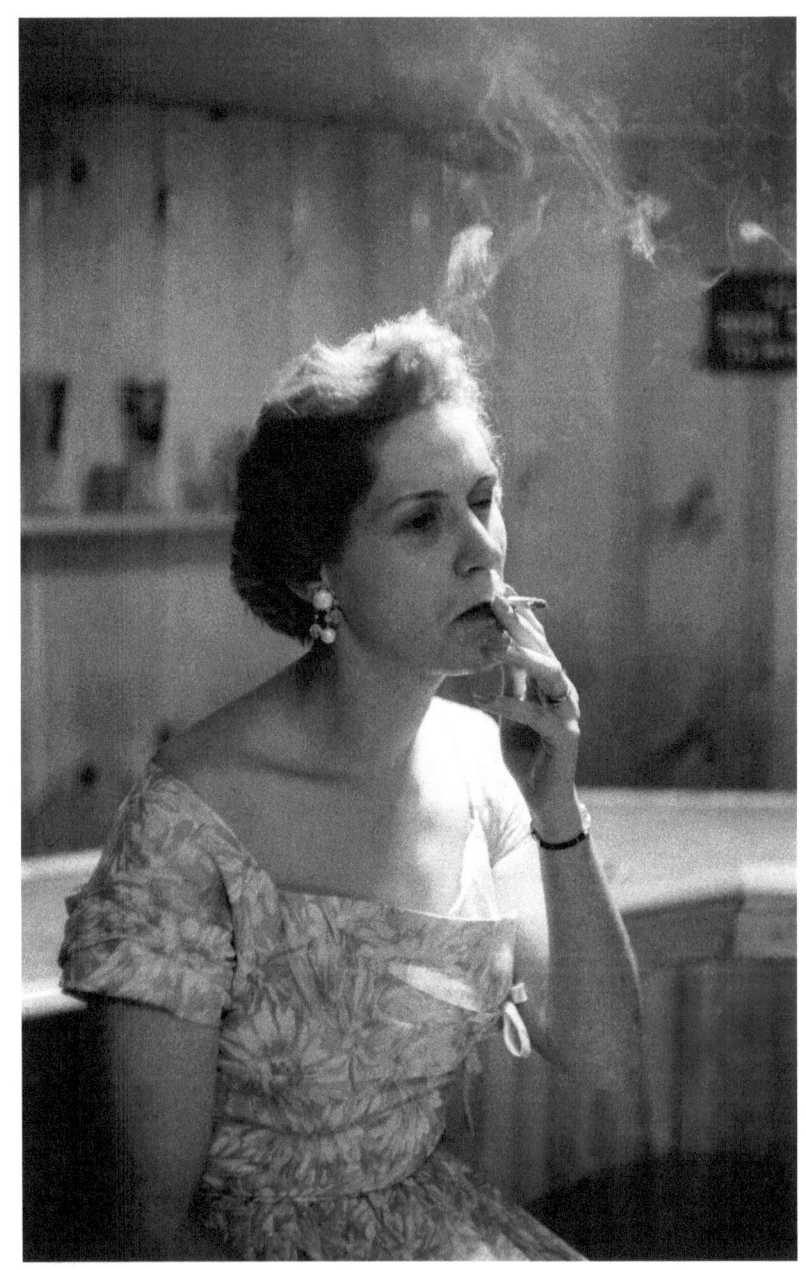

Drag *Alliance, Ohio 1956*

Not only were the factories and my photography smoking, so were the people. The advertising industry promoted cigarettes everywhere, and some ads carried testimonials from physicians on the alleged health benefits of smoking. It was touted as an aid to dieting and as an end-of-day "pick-me-up." Women were encouraged to be more fashionable, and men more manly, with the right cigarette.

Smoking

Some high-school boys thought it was "cool" to wear their white tee shirts with one sleeve neatly rolled to create a pocket for a pack of smokes. We weren't calling them "coffin nails" yet. Most people smoked, and we thought nothing of it.

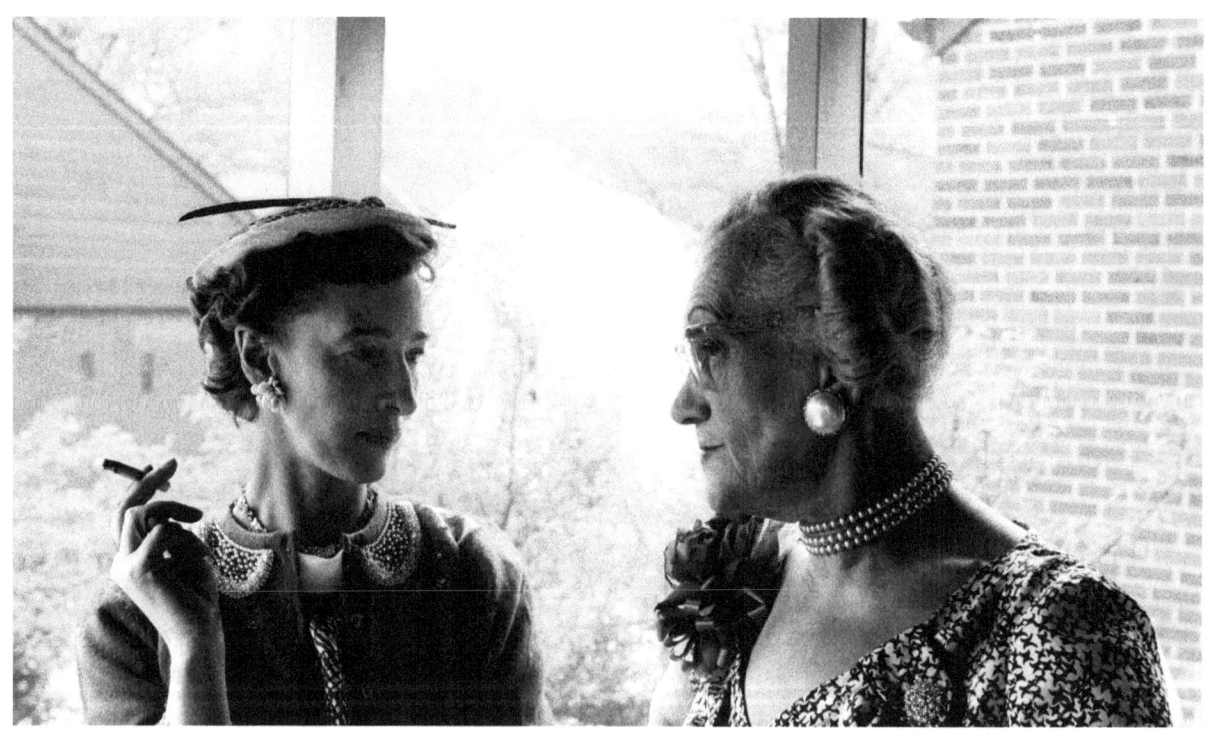

Chat *Alliance, Ohio 1956*

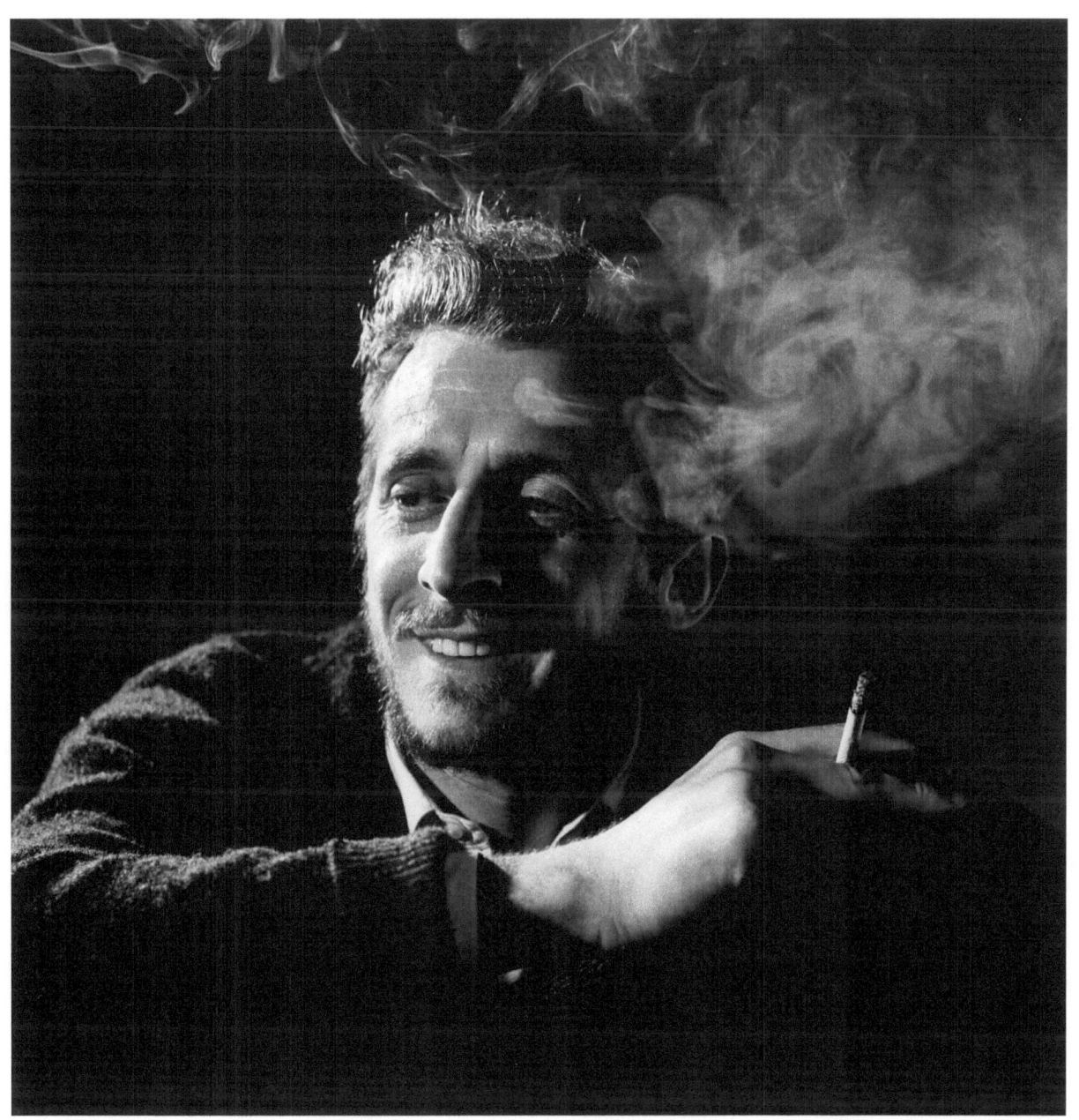

Balduzzi *Alliance, Ohio 1957*

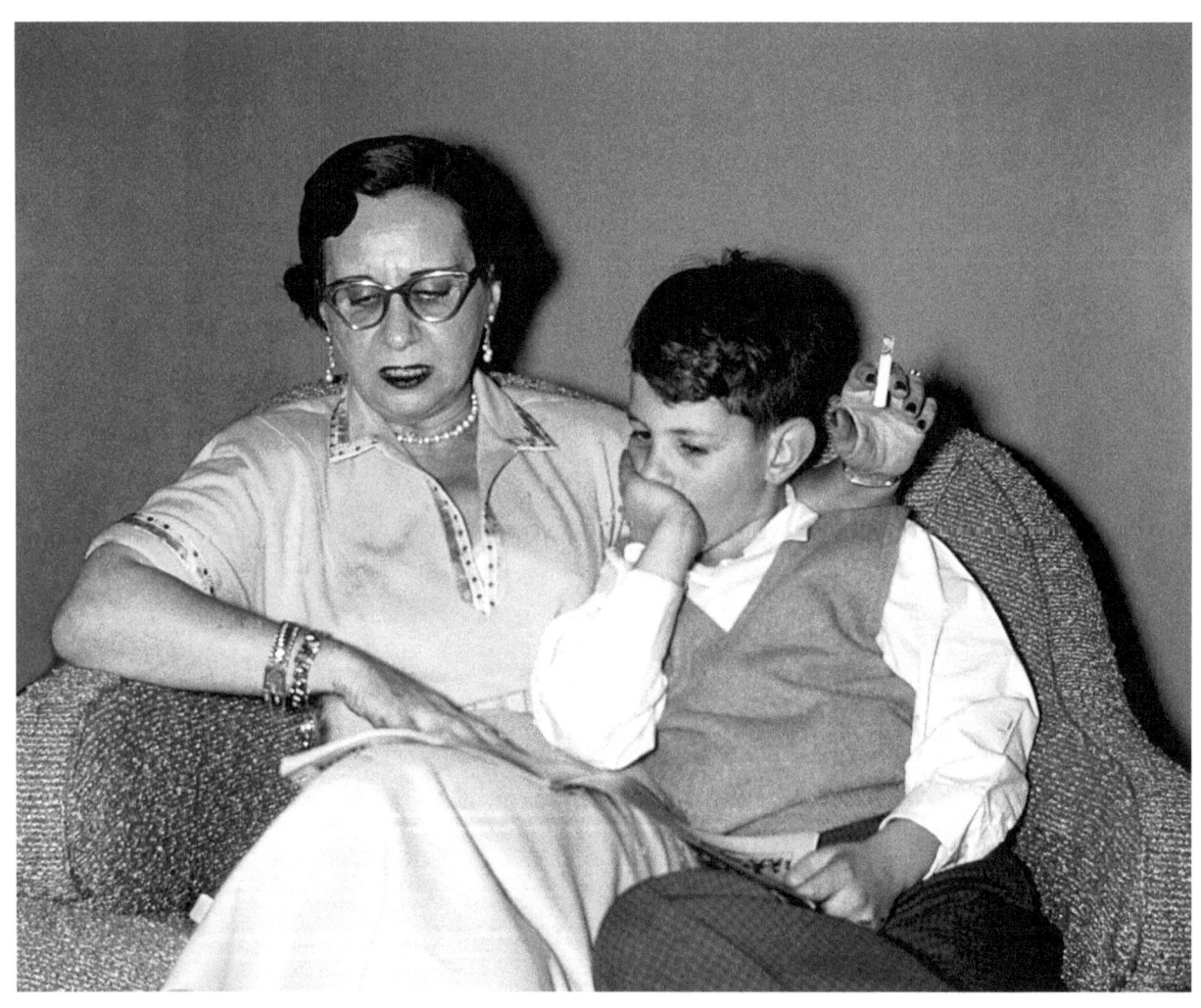

Smoking Story *Alliance, Ohio 1955*

Some of us moved out and on.

Graduating high school for some meant enrolling in college. For others it was graduating into a factory job that pulled in the big bucks for the time, enough to make a payment on the newest model of car.

Happy days that included waterskiing in Ohio transitioned into city life for me, university dorms, and rowing in an eight-man shell for my sport. Now I was leaving behind memories that went back to my elementary school days. I thought my silent goodbyes to high school and all the local photography, embracing even the "dear hearts" who went to luncheons and whose universe was so different from my own.

Transition

Throughout it all, I was oblivious to being part of the scene. I recently heard that when you are a little kid, you don't question how things are, because that's just how it is. Well, that's how it was, and it took a lot of growing up for myself.

New friends offered new experiences, as did documenting life in a fresh scene, in and around Philadelphia. There was also more smoking, to which I was indifferent; I never got the hang of it, except for creating interesting photo compositions.

I supplemented my Wharton School formal education with a self-created, unofficial minor in photojournalism. I took writing courses from newspaper and magazine pros, figuring that those skills would help me market my photographs. And I photographed constantly, on self-assignments and for the University yearbook and newspaper.

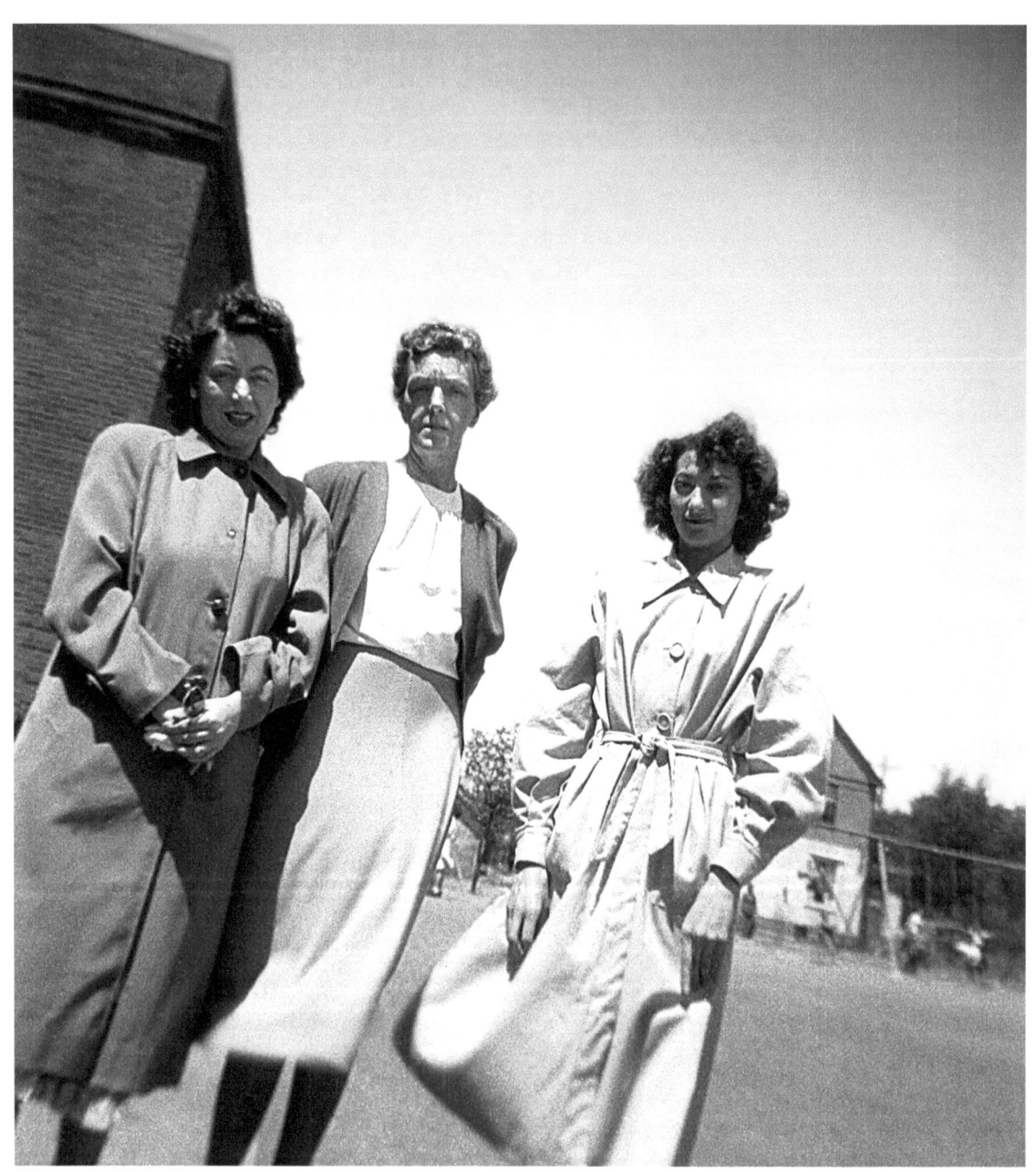

Towering Teachers *Alliance, Ohio 1947*

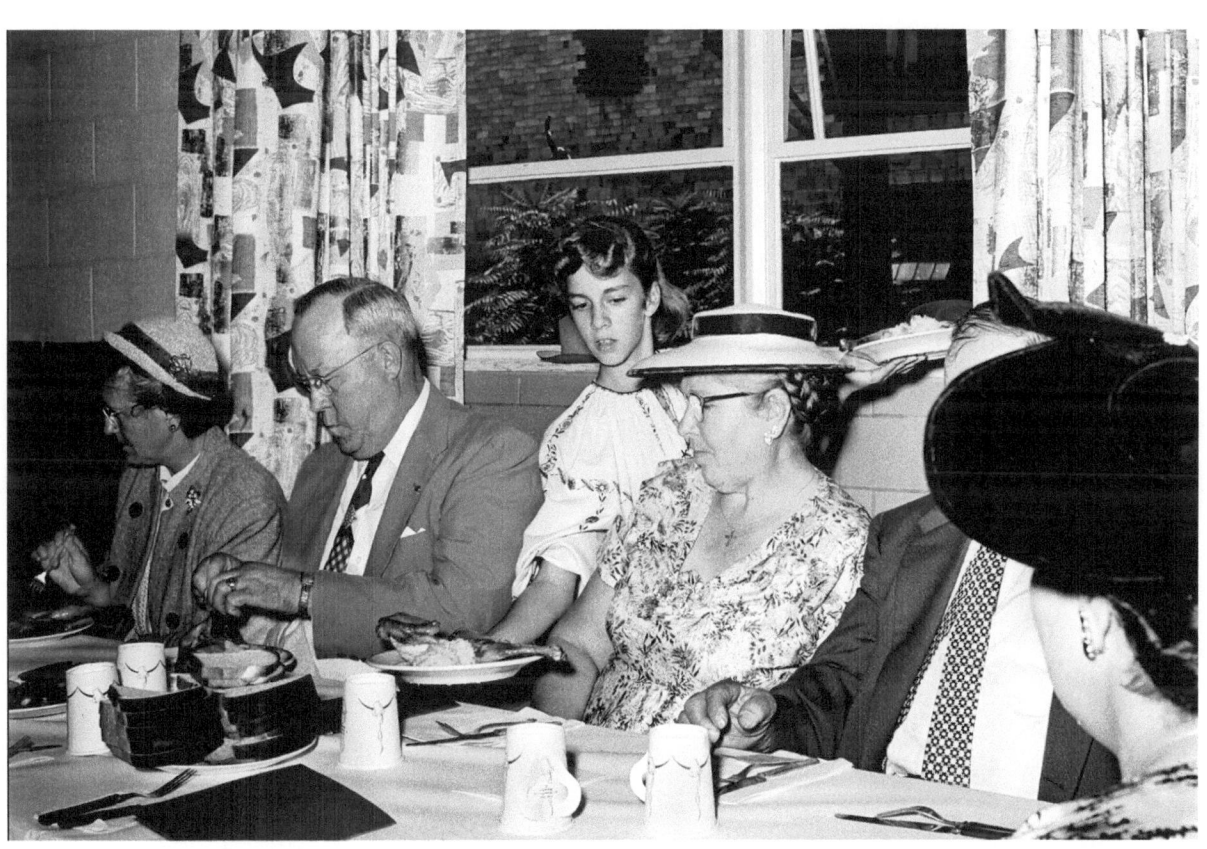

Ladies in Hats *Alliance, Ohio 1955*

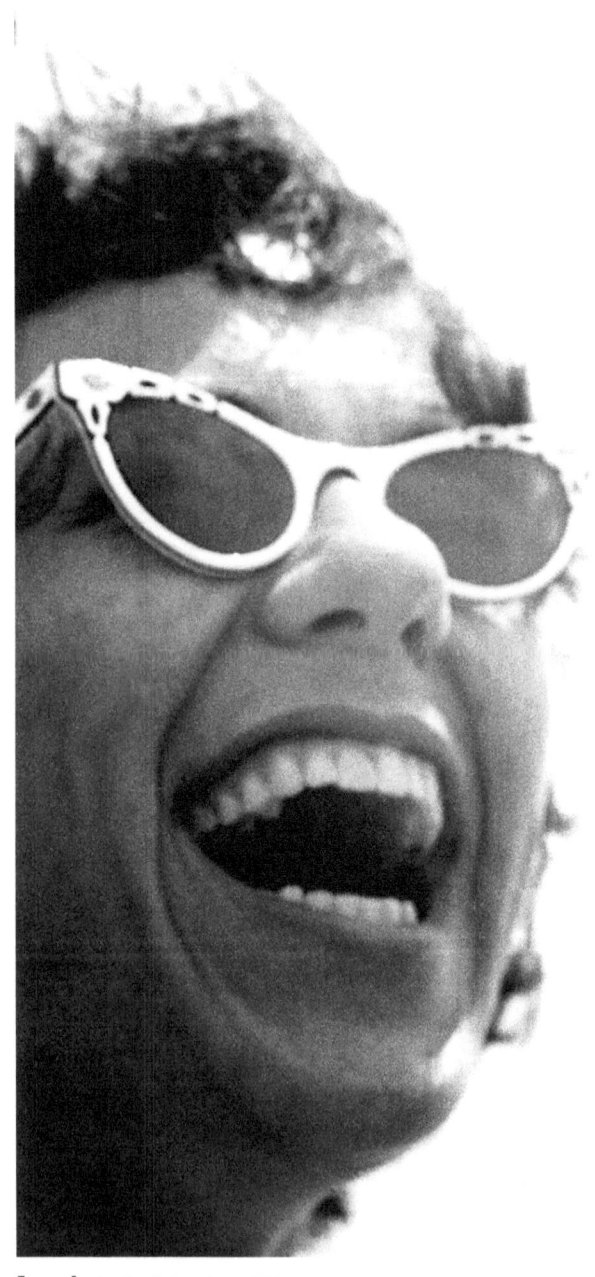

Laugh *Berlin Lake, Ohio 1959*

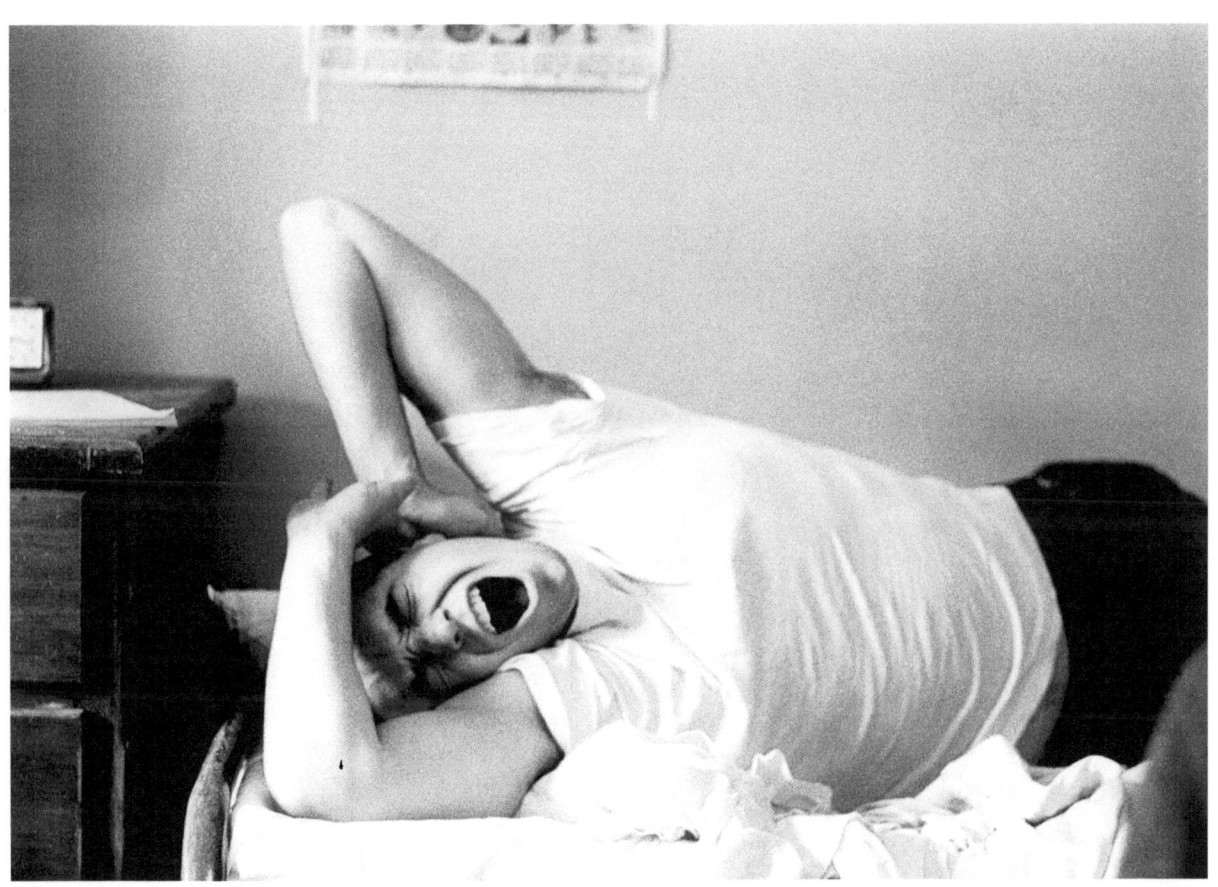

Yawn *Philadelphia, Pennsylvania 1956*

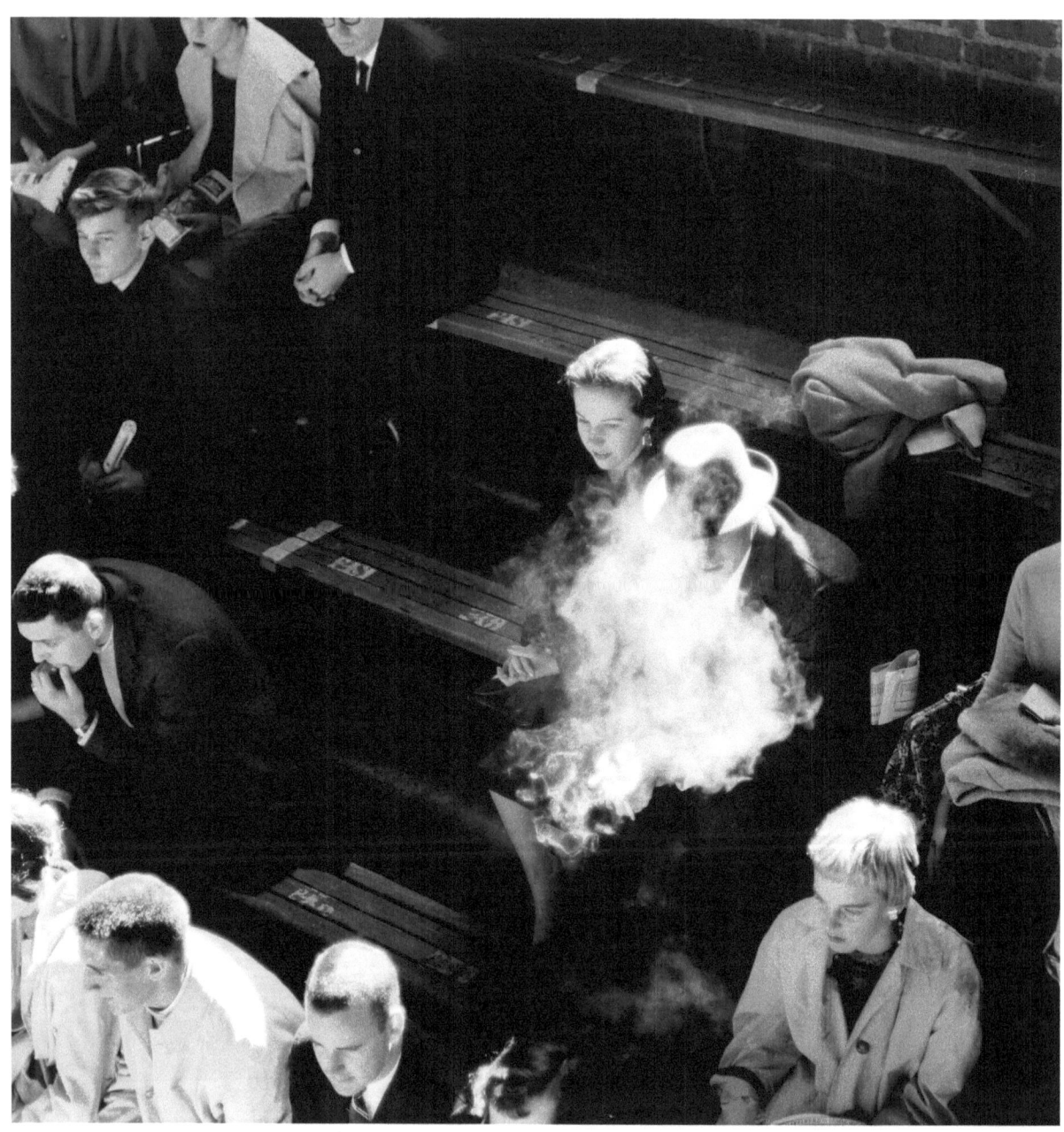

Smokescreen *Philadelphia, Pennsylvania 1959*

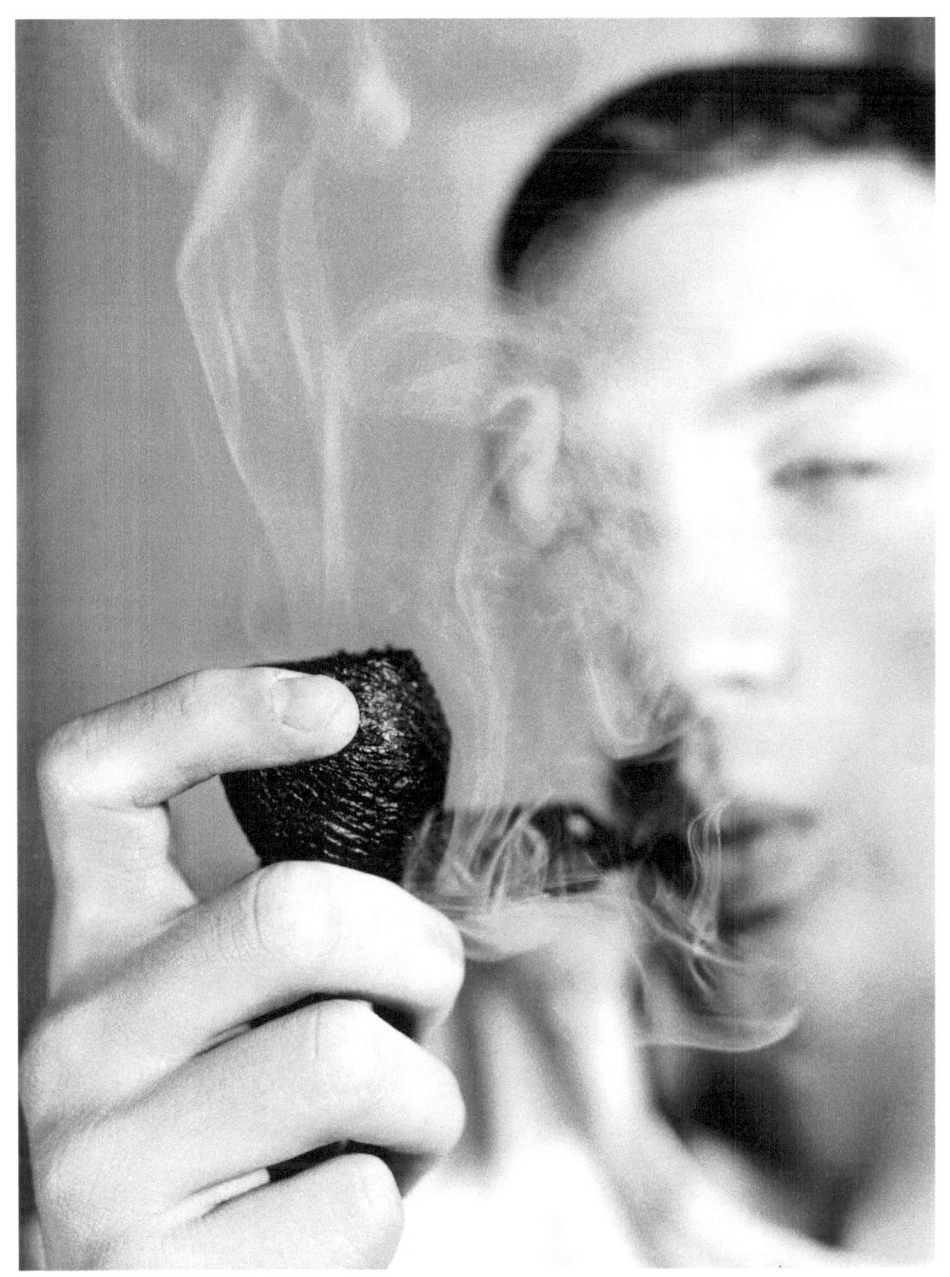

Pipe Dream *Philadelphia, Pennsylvania 1958*

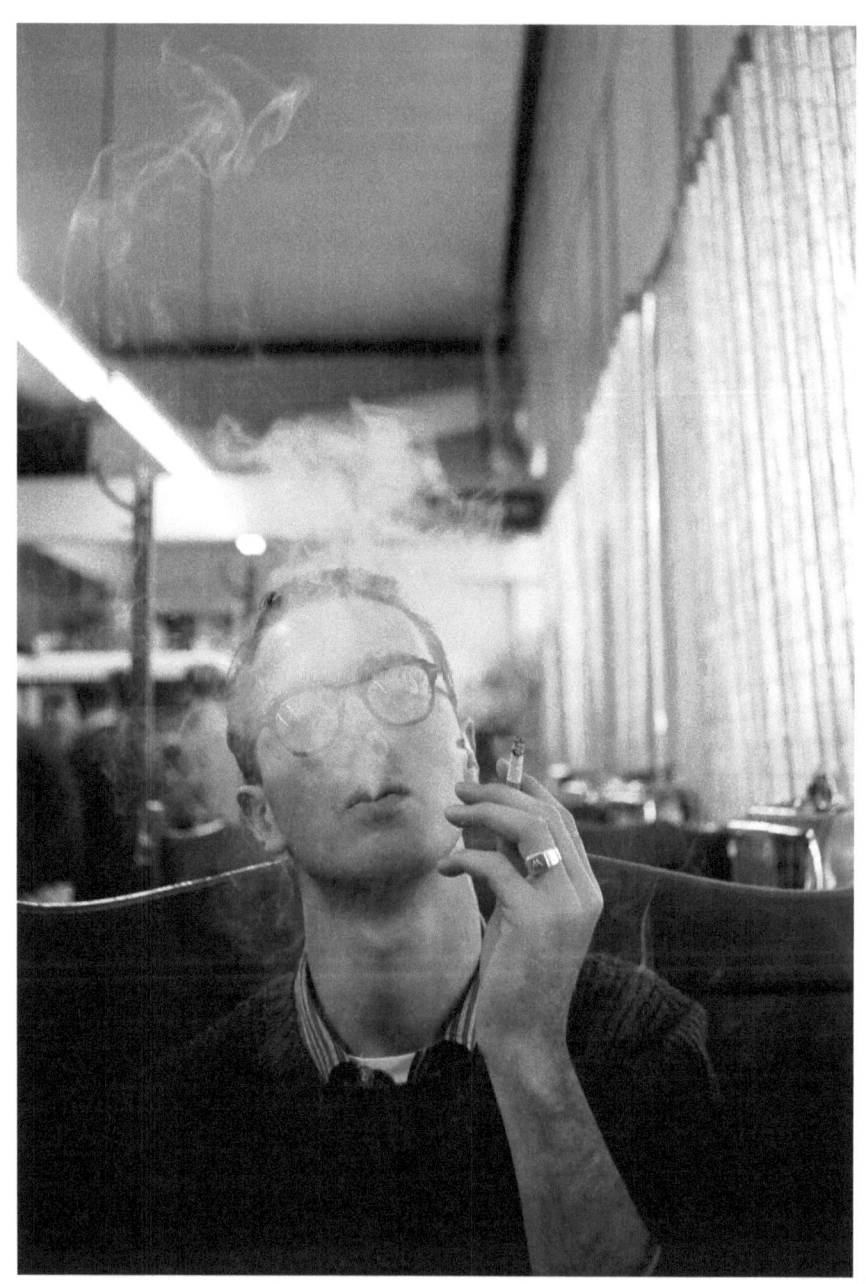

Café Smoker *Philadelphia, Pennsylvania 1958*

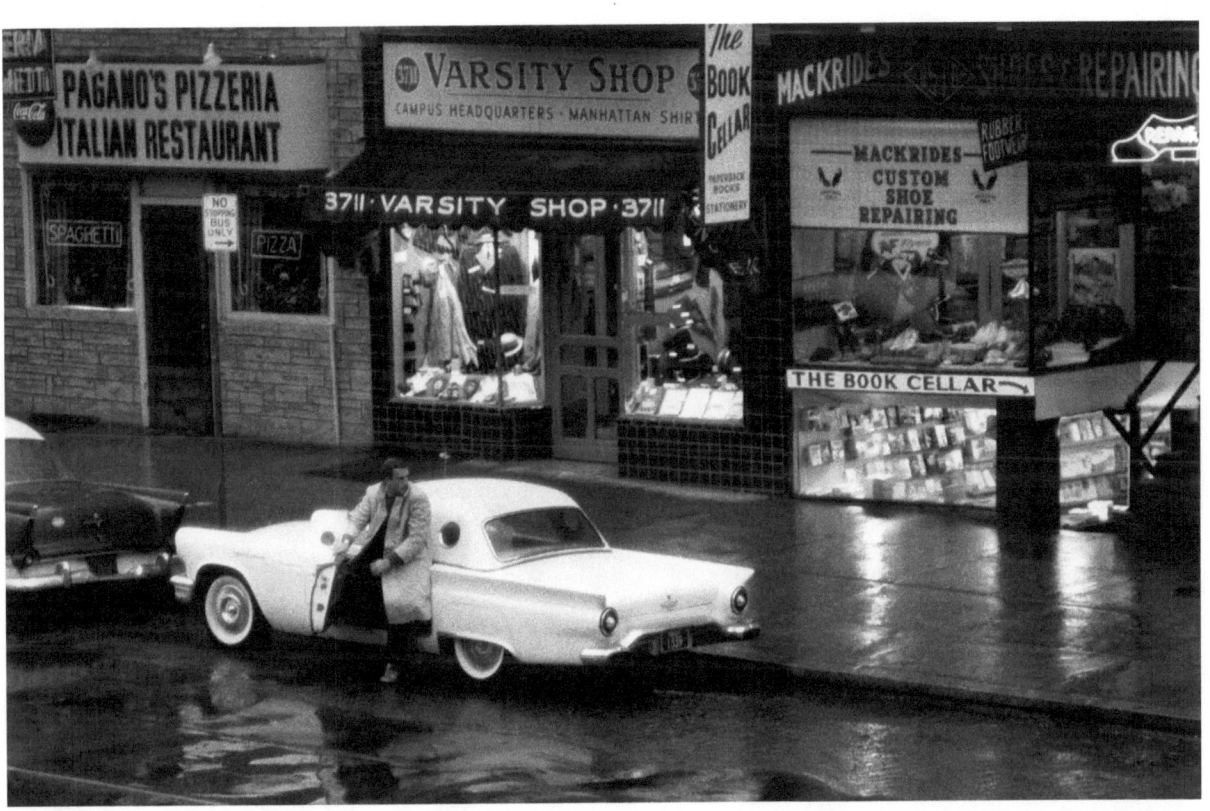

'57 T-Bird *Philadelphia, Pennsylvania 1958*

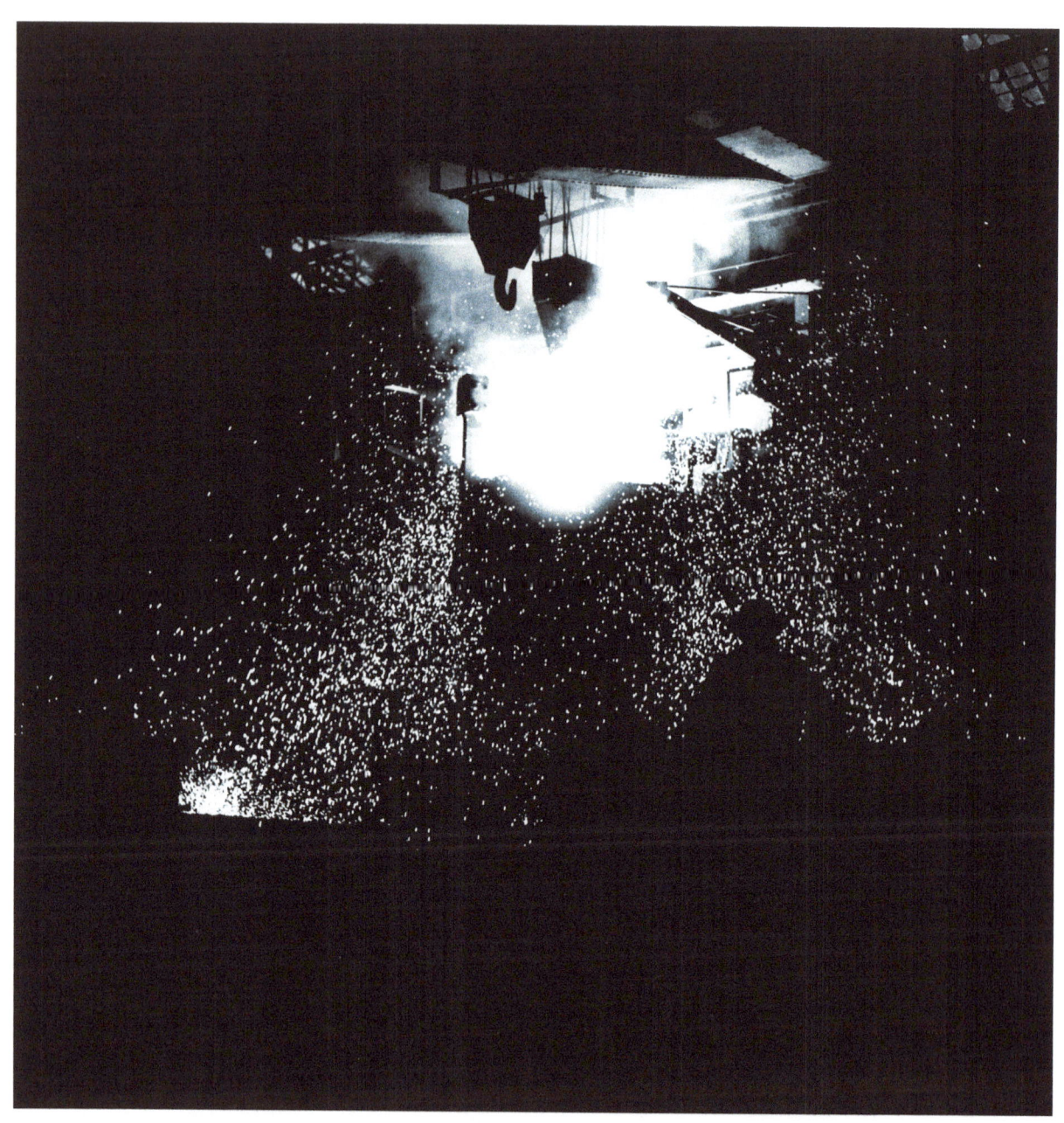

Steel Sparks *Alliance, Ohio 1957*

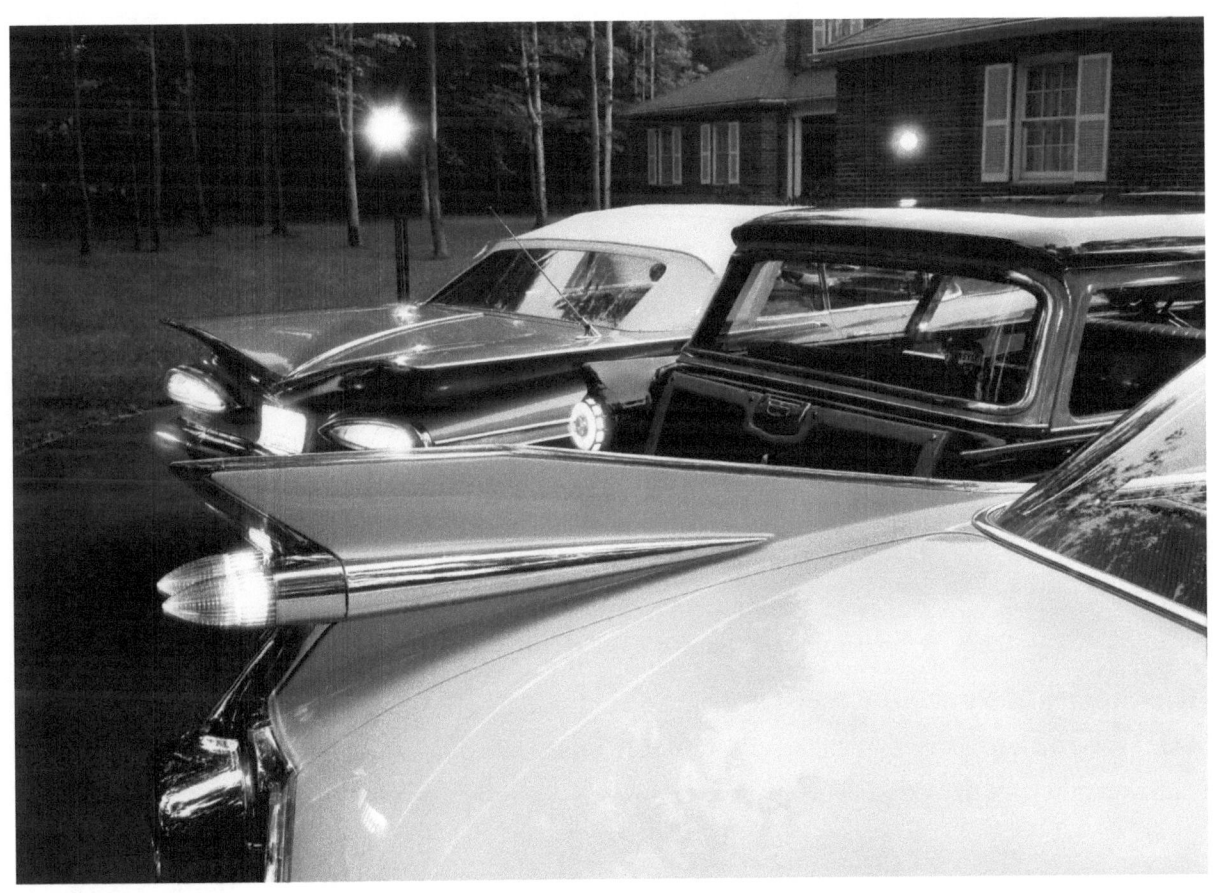

Fins in the Fifties *Alliance, Ohio 1959*

Epilogue

Here at home, Americans could finally rejoice in the present, while mourning our dead and helping to confront incredible chaos abroad. I recently met a 17-year-old student of history named Faith. She remarked that all had been irrationally peaceful here "before the war became America's problem."

With the bombing of Pearl Harbor, the U.S. could no longer ignore what was happening abroad, and had no alternative but to join in. And the aftermath? The world had to deal with the effects of genocide and the monumental problems of displaced persons. Millions of people had died, millions were homeless. Cities in Europe and Asia were reduced to rubble, with economies destroyed. The United States pitched in, once again, and billions of dollars went for reconstruction and resettlement.

I was five years old when World War II ended, and was aware only of my own childhood. I learned what happened later on, through family photographs, genealogy, discussions, reading and travel. Most of my great-aunts and uncles in Hungary had been slaughtered or enslaved. A few encountered good Samaritans who risked their own lives to help.

Many years ago, when exiting the Holocaust museum at Dachau in Germany, I was faced with a quote from philosopher George Santayana. It was painted in large letters on the wall at the door. As memory serves, it read like this:

"Those who cannot remember the past are condemned to repeat it."

I hope that quote is still there. I hope that enough political leaders can right the wrongs of the chaos of today. I gain hope, as we mobilize to maintain the gains we have made. And I gain further hope as Faith and others of her generation expand upon an awareness that will serve humanity in the years ahead.

— Michael Philip Manheim

IMAGE INSIGHTS

Michael Philip Manheim

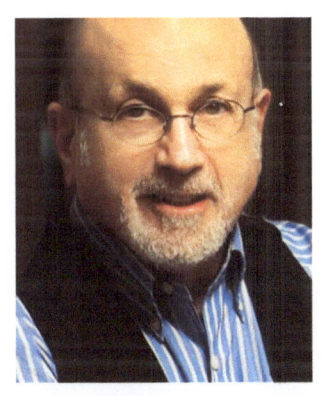

Manheim is widely recognized both for his documentary and for his innovative multiple exposure photographs. Both categories encompass images that promote feelings. Most celebrate human emotion as a primal link that unifies all of humankind.

Michael Philip Manheim's photography has been exhibited throughout the United States and internationally, in over 20 solo exhibitions and 30 group shows. His work has been featured extensively online, as well as in hundreds of books and magazines such as *Zoom* (U.S. and Italy), *Photographers International* (Taiwan), *La Fotografia* (Spain), and *Black and White Magazine* (U.S.).

Manheim's photographs are held in private as well as public collections including the Library of Congress, the International Photography Hall of Fame, the National Archives, the Danforth Museum of Art, and the Bates College Museum of Art.

Photograph courtesy of Scott Hershovitz

www.ingramcontent.com/pod-product-compliance
Lightning Source LLC
Chambersburg PA
CBHW050901180526
45159CB00007B/2752